CUSTER WENT FIRST

Custer Went First

By Kerry G. Lundmark

XULON PRESS

MCP Books
2301 Lucien Way #415
Maitland, FL 32751
407.339.4217
www.MCPBooks.com

Printed in the United States of America

ISBN-13: 9781545603390

Contents

Introduction

Custer went first. As was the custom and training of the United States Cavalry in 1876, the heads of military columns of troops were led by the senior commanders. Lieutenant Colonel (brevet Major-General) George Armstrong Custer led his troops on that fateful day, June 25, 1876. Today most literature and historical accounts refer to that day as Custer's Last Stand. It was also known as the Custer Battlefield on the Little Bighorn River in Montana.

Most novices to the battle recall it as a quick battle of annihilation of the 7th Cavalry by an overwelming body of Indians. Over time the accounts of the battle have become accounts of exonercation or blame to be hung about the heads of General Custer himself; his second-in-command, Major (brevet Brigadier- General) Marcus Reno; or his third-in-command, Captain (brevet Colonel) Frederick Benteen.

What is known is the story recorded from interviews and a military court of inquiry by participants who survived the battles. These thoughts and memories of witnesses to the battle and their written observations were made after the battle, but the testimony and recorded recollections still live on. The diverse views and contradictions make the one story of truth difficult to determine. Over time these accounts have been colored and used to accuse or vindicate those who fought that day.

Whether American Indian or soldier, retribution by an American population was foremost in the telling of the story of the battles that day. Indians were being hunted, killed, or forced onto reservations, where daily sustenance was always at risk. Soldiers and their careers were under scrutiny by their superiors and by the president himself. Newspapers were attacking and accusing anyone and everyone who had anything to do with the greatest U.S. Army defeat since the days of the Civil War. Justice had to be served, but who's justice, and for what purpose?

As I researched and read the accounts and histories of the Indian survivors and the soldier accounts, I was most taken by the lack of cohesion in the many stories and the battlefield's layout as seen today. Many have tried to recreate the movements of the 7th Cavalry during and leading up to the battle. However, from my reading of the Indian and soldier accounts, no one has put together a realistic picture of what happened to the five companies that died with Custer that day.

Some will say it can never be done, as all died. But still, a story did happen that day. The relics of battle, the bodies found on the battlefield, and the survivor accounts do provide significant pieces to the puzzle. A reasonable narrative of the end of those five companies can be surmised. If one does not try to color the witness accounts to condemn or justify, an amazingly simple and honest chronology of events can be discerned. A story as to how those five companies, those 200 or so soldiers, died that day in 1876 can be told.

In addition to the dead soldiers, many American Indians died or were wounded on the Little Bighorn, or the Greasy Grass, as they called it. American Indians viewed battles in a more personal way than the soldiers view. To these participants, the battles that day were many, and were like a large buffalo hunt. Accounts of personal bravery and honors scored by touching enemies, counting coup, created the memories of the day.

No Indian accounts record flanking movements or planned tactics to counter soldier threats. Rather, the day was one of rallying to threatened ends of the large Indian camp and fighting many soldier *wasichu*. Eventually at the end of that day, the twenty-fifth of June, 1876, one large area of the banks of the Little Bighorn was covered with dead soldiers and their horses. Four miles away, on a separate hill, soldiers gathered in a defensive circle waiting for reinforcement. By either General Custer and his contingent, or by the large contingent under the command of the campaign leader, Brigadier- General Alfred Terry, help and hope was eagarly anticipated

So why another book about a battle fought so long ago? When I first visited the battlefield in 1992, the many headstones on the grounds showed where soldiers had died. The story at the time was that these soldiers had been routed. They died in what seemed to be less- than-heroic manners. Yet four miles away to the south was another setting where soldiers within the same command, with the same training, same discipline, had formed a tight defensive perimeter and dug in. They survived the onslaught the next day by the same Indians that had wiped out their comrades the day before. How could that be?

When I walked the landscape in 1992 I noted many markers inscribed with the words, "U. S. Soldier, 7th Cavalry, Fell Here, June 25, 1876." I felt an unsettled emptiness thinking that young men with names, families, histories, were all left to be forgotten, their true story of resistance and actions were left to self-serving soldier and civilian agendas. This, at best, seemed to be unfair.

There were survivors and their accounts were recorded. For the soldiers there were field reports. A formal Court of Inquiry into the actions of Major Reno was held by the Army in Chicago in early 1879. The minutes of those proceedings are available for all to read today.

From 1935 through 1957, one David Humphreys Miller went to talk with American Indians who had participated in that battle. He recorded the Indian stories and released books featuring their side of the battle. The Indian memories are quite specific on who was seen and what honors they achieved that day.

There were later-year newspaper interviews with the old soldiers and the Crow and Arikara Indian scouts who had ridden with Custer that day. Each story, each interview, holds precious clues on the actions of the five companies of cavalry that perished that day.

Sometimes the testimonies seem to be in conflict. Over time many of these conflicting stories were either ignored or dismissed as unreasonable. Yet each of the authors, these witnesses, did “see” and or “hear” the battles. The clues in their memories like testimony in a courtroom reveal a common unified story of truth.

Many soldiers referenced their testimony to places indicated on a crucial map produced by a Lieutenent Edward Maguire. Maguire’s map and his report of the battlefields was ordered by Brigadier-General Alfred Terry on June 28, 1876. General Terry was about to leave the scene with the wounded and surviving members of the fight. Lieutenant Maguire, as part of the Corps of Engineers assigned to the campaign, did a commendable job with Sergeant Charles Becker in detailing areas of the battles. When compared to overhead aerial camera shots of the area today, his detail has remarkable accuracies. At the same time, large areas to the east of the high bluffs were left as uncharted and unmapped. This map was used by the Reno Court of Inquiry time and time again to describe the movements of the 7th Cavalry that day in 1876. When reading the testimonies of men from 1879 and using this map, stories become clearer. When comparing current topographical maps and aerial maps to this discussion, the movements of the five companies that perished that day can be determined with a fair amount of accuracy.

Archeological findings since then have added more detail to the fighting. One significant finding was on a nearby ridge known as Blummer or Nye-Cartwright. Spent shells of the calibre used by the 7th Cavalry were found on the ridge. This site was not known to the Reno Court of Inquiry (RCOI). Yet rereading the RCOI testimonies with this key piece of knowledge provides clearer understanding of the northern battles.

To visit the Little Bighorn River (LBH) site today, the National Park Service has designated two sites as being the current battle field arenas. But in following the testimonies and reviewing the locations of the dead as marked on the battlefield, I have determined there were actually nine battles that constituted the Battle of the Little Bighorn.

Three of these engagements are well documented by the surviving companies on the southern end of the Little Bighorn Battlefield. To the north, there were an additional six engagements. These I shall describe and offer a most plausible reason for what happened at each.

Furthermore, the identification of the Custer Battlefield was changed by the National Park Service to the Little Bighorn Battlefield to account for American Indian participation. I myself will use designations as the southern Reno-Benteen Hill (R/B) site, and the northern Yates-Keogh battle sites. Many geographic features will be referred to as these are key in the testimonies.

To those of you unfamiliar with the battle, its background, and details, the following chapters will explain how the day went. To those of you with more detailed knowledge of the battle my major discussions on the movements of the five lost companies will begin in Chapter Six. My hope is that the reader will gain a more complete, more human understanding of the decisions made and the consequences of those decisions.

Like modern-day accident investigations done by the National Transportation and Safety Board (NTSB), most catastrophes are not the result of one major bad decision. Rather a series of smaller decisions made when confronted by an unplanned action alters the entire day. That is what transpired on June 25, 1876. A planned action of the part of General George Custer was severely interrupted at the onset. Subsequent actions and decisions were made that cost the lives of over 200 troopers and many American Indian participants.

The Battle of the Little Bighorn was significant to the development of the northern plains of the United States. The completion of the Great Northern Railroad by James J. Hill and the competing Northern Pacific Railroad would lead to the subsequent development of the states of North and South Dakota, Montana, and Wyoming.

The industrial expansion from Minnesota to Puget Sound in the then Washington Territory would provide economic as well as political motivations that would force this battle. It would become an inevitable confrontation with the American Indians of the Northern Plains. The end to the wild and free lifestyle of the Plains Indians came about because of this battle. Legends and myths and family histories would forever be altered and become a part of Western Americanna.

George Armstrong Custer would become a soldier hero or a foolish lunatic soldier both at the same time. The verdict to be decided if one was defending General Custer or accusing and deriding him. But the stories of the dead, the "Unknowns," designated "U. S. Soldier, 7th Cavalry, Fell Here, June 25, 1876," would forever be overshadowed by the desires of legend makers and legend breakers. This was to be a Custer day of destiny. I hope to restore some of the dignity to those quiet unknowns who rest eternally on that hillside of the Little Bighorn River.

Mysteries remain even to this day. The participants whether white man or Indian, never forgot those two days of battle. Horrific images of personal struggles and chaos would cloud the battle memories. Of the twelve companies of troopers that made up the 7th Cavalry Regiment then, six saw their commanding officers killed on that twenty-fifth day of June, 1876. Five companies lost their second-in-command leaders. A little-known fact is that of the five annihlated companies not every trooper of those companies was killed that day. In fact some were assigned by General Custer to other duties with the pack-train.

Then as now, officers were to be with their men. They were to guide and lead them during the battle. However, of the six commanding company officers killed that day, two were not found with their companies on the battlefield. Of the second-in-command officers of the five decimated companies, three were not found with their companies.

Though the bodies of all company commanders were discovered after the battle, the bodies of the three subordinate officers were never found or recovered. Where did they end up and why? Why were two of the company commanders not with their troops at the end? Why could seven companies of the 7th Cavalry survive while five companies could not? They fought the same Indians, the same overwelming numbers of warriors and braves. Why did the five companies fail? Did General George Armstrong Custer have a plan of action that day? Was he truly unaware of the large number of Indians before him? How could he possibly expect to win the day with his twelve companies of troopers? General Custer was under military arrest by order of President Grant at the time of his demise. Did this force Custer to make hasty and risky decisions to save his career? Or did the mystical Indian *Wakan Tanka*, Father Spirit, guide the troopers to their death on the hills of the Greasy Grass?

To date, many books have been written on the subject. Much is known of the southern battles of the Little Bighorn from the survivors of that part of the battlefield. But the battles of the northern end have been left to archeologists and the interpretation of tales from Indians. Today if a visitor wishes to see the battlefields, they will walk those two separate fields under the protection of the National Park Service.

The sequence of these battles is crucial to determine the actions that ended the lives of the five companies on the northern end of the Little Bighorn Battlefield. Most historians have come to regard the final movements of those five companies of cavalry as lost to the fog of war. But some amazingly accurate detail of those actions can be found in the recorded testimonies of participants who survived.

Obviously there are the accounts of the Indians who were victorious that day to be taken into consideration. On the side of the cavalry there were four troopers and four Crow Indian scouts who had important clues as to how the battles in the northern end unfolded.

Much detail has been written of the battles that occurred on the southern end. There were in fact three major separate actions there. The first being a charge and skirmish in the river valley of the Little Bighorn River by three companies led by Major Marcus Reno, second-in-command of the 7th Cavalry that day. The second battle of the southern end occurred when a company commander, Captain Thomas Weir, advanced to a high hill today known as Weir Point. Seven companies advanced to this hill under the command of Major Reno: Reno's three companies, three companies under the command of Captain Frederick Benteen, and the company charged with protection of the pack mule train, Company B. The pack-train and Company B was under the command of Captain Thomas McDougall. Captain Benteen was the senior-most captain and thus third by rank in chanrge of the 7th Cavalry. At Weir Point they all were attacked by the Indians who had only recently defeated the five companies on the northern end.

These seven companies retreated from Weir Point to the area of the current southern field of the Little Bighorn Battlefield National Monument. Here they formed a tight circle of defense and fought through the evening of June 25th, and most of the day on the 26th in the third and final southern battle.

On the morning of the 27th, these companies were rescued by the column of troops under the overall command of Brigadier General Alfred Terry and Colonel John Gibbon. It was during June 27th and 28th that much of the evidence of the battle was detailed. Bodies of the dead were buried where they were found.

These burials were marked originally with primitive markers. The officers were identified and their burial sites marked with their names. All other troopers were buried with markers denoting "UNKNOWN."

Before Terry's column left the battlefields with the wounded, General Terry ordered Lieutenant Edward Maguire, an Army Engineer, to make a survey of the battlefield. This map was to be used for later reference to the battles in Lieutenant Maguire's formal report to the Corps of Engineers in July 1876.

This map was the key reference used two and a half years later during the Reno Court of Inquiry held by the U.S. Army during January and Februry 1879 in Chicago. It was during these proceedings that much of the testimony of surviving Army participants was formally recorded.

Unfortunately these proceedings were in a politically charged environment. Major Reno was being accused of cowardice and actions unbecoming an officer, namely being drunk while commanding his troops in battle. A pro-Custer newsman, Frederick Whittaker, had accused Reno and Benteen of deserting Custer and failing to save his command.

President Ulysses Grant was under fire for not properly dealing with the hostile Indians of the Plains and for corruption on the Army posts by profiteers. This included charges made by Custer in the spring of 1876 about President Grant's brother Orvil.

President Grant's friends General William Tecumseh Sherman, general-in-command of the Army, and Lieutenant-General Philip Sheridan, adjutant- general of the military division of the Missouri, were being hard pressed to explain the failure of the Army in this battle. Conflicting views of the battle and the conduct of the Army were being circulated in the newspapers and military reports. Major Reno, feeling pressure both within the military ranks and from newspaper attacks, requested that a court of inquiry into his actions at the battle be established.

In reading the proceedings today, if one can take an objective look at the testimony of the twenty-three witnesses, inconsistent statements can be reconciled. By tying the statements to current topographic maps and the Maguire map, a few educated guesses can be made as to what happened to the five companies. The Reno Court of Inquiry (RCOI) did not hear any of the Indian witness accounts. Actions of troopers on the nearby ridge now known as Nye-Cartwright (Blummer) Ridge were not understood until the 1920s when cartridges were found there in significant quantities. By using archeologic evaluations from this location, it is known some of the five companies Custer led participated in the battles from here.

Significant to the RCOI proceedings was the knowledge that Custer had divided his regiment into battalions for action against the Indians. Major Reno commanded one battalion of three companies: A, M, and G. Captain Frederick Benteen was placed in command of another battalion of three companies: H, D, and K. Custer assigned one company, B, to Captain Thomas McDougall to guard the pack-train of mules with supplies including extra ammunition boxes. Custer retained five companies under his command. These were divided into two battalions. One battalion of three companies- I, L, and C- was led by Captain Myles Keogh. The other battalion of two companies- F and E- was led by Captain George Yates.

Yates' battalion was reduced in strength to two companies when Custer assigned Company B to the pack-train. Captain Keogh was senior to Captain Yates. All twelve companies had been reduced from a normal compliment of about fifty men each by Custer. He had ordered one non-commisioned officer (NCO) and six troopers from each company to be assigned to the protection of the pack-train under Captain McDougall's command.

Two companies, Company E and Company C, hold particular interest for understanding the northern battles. Company E, led by First Lieutenant Algernon Smith and Second Lieutenant. James Sturgis, was unique in the horses they rode. While eleven companies rode brown cavalry horses, Company E rode gray horses. These had been reassigned by Custer from the band back at Fort Lincoln, located outside of Bismarck. These horses were assigned to this company so as to complete a full compliment of twelve companies for this campaign.

Surviving witnesses soldier and Indian alike- recalled seeing troops of the gray horse company during the battles on the 25th. Second Lieutenant Sturgis, second-in-command of Company E, was son to Colonel Sturgis, the senior commander of the 7th Cavalry, though for the campaign, General Terry had requested Custer head up the regiment due to his previous experience fighting Indians. Lieutenant Sturgis was an infantryman by training, on temporary assignment to the 7th Cavalry from the 20th Infantry Regiment.

Company C was commanded by Captain Thomas Ward Custer, brother to George Custer. He and his second-in-command, Second Lieutenant Henry Harrington, shared Company C duties. Quite often Captain Custer, a twice-honored Civil War Medal of Honor recipient, was seen riding with the advanced scouts and with his brother George. Captain Tom Custer regularly called his brother by his nickname, Autie. Often they were out front of the column by some distance. Thus, much of the Company C command duties fell upon Lieutenant Harrington.

These two companies had distinct differences from the other three companies that perished that day. The troopers of these companies died in their final battle locations with neither their commanding officer nor their second-in-commanding officer with them. No reasonable explanation that fit with the other actions on the battlefield seemed to be found. The company commanders of these two companies died on Last Stand Hill far from the rest of their commands. Why? The second-in-command officers of Company E and Company C disappeared, not to be found on the battlefield. Again, why?

Other mysteries remained. What happened to First Lieutenant James Porter, second-in-command of Company I? Why was Sergeant James Butler of Company L found separated from his company? Why did there seem to be two separate tracks of retreating soldiers from the river ford where the Medicine Tail Coulee meets the Little Bighorn River as shown on the Maguire map? Why did they go north and not south to meet the reinforcements of Captain Benteen's battalion, or east to escape the onrushing Indians?

To many these remaining mysteries were of small or little consequence. But in trying to find a story that explains them and the generally known deaths of the five companies, a new study was needed. It is in the re-reading of the soldier and Indian accounts that clues were offered to these unknown endings. The battles on the north end of the Little Bighorn Battlefield were fought in a progression, and as the progression of the fighting took place, a significant question arose, one which was asked at the Reno Court of Inquiry in 1879:

"State whether or not in your opinion, General Custer could have fled the field with a portion of his command by abandoning the others to their fate?" This key question was asked only once by the Reno Court of Inquiry, and then only addressed to Second Lieutenant Winfield Edgerly, second-in-command of Company D, who was with the Benteen battalion. It was never answered directly. Lieutenant Edgerly politely responded, "He fought very desperately."

1

Orders, Reports, and News

Headquarters Department of Dakota, (In the Field)

Camp at the Mouth of Rosebud River, Montana, June 22, 1876

Colonel: The Brigadier-General commanding directs that as soon as your regiment can be made ready for the march, you proceed up the Rosebud in pursuit of the Indians whose trail was discovered by Major Reno a few days since. It is, of course, impossible to give you any definite instructions in regard to this movement; and were it not impossible to do so, the department commander places too much confidence in your zeal, energy, and ability to wish to impose upon you precise orders, which might hamper your action when nearly in contact with the enemy. He will, however, indicate to you his own desires that you should conform to them unless you shall see sufficient reason for departing from them. He thinks that you should proceed up the Rosebud until you ascertain definitely the direction in which the trail above spoken of leads. Should it be found (as it appears to be almost certain that it will be found) to turn toward the Little Horn, he thinks that you should still proceed

southward, perhaps as far as the headwaters of the Tongue, and then turn toward the Little Horn, feeling constantly, however, to your left, so as to preclude the possibility of the escape of the Indians to the south or southeast by passing around your left flank.

The column of Colonel Gibbon is now in motion for the mouth of the Big Horn. As soon as it reaches that point it will cross the Yellowstone and move up at least as far as the forks of the Little and Big Horns. Of course its future movements must be controlled by circumstances as they arise; but it is hoped that the Indians if upon the Little Horn, may be so nearly enclosed by the two columns that their escape will be impossible. The department commander desires that on your way up the Rosebud you should thoroughly examine the upper part of Tullock's Creek; and that you should endeavor to send a scout through to Colonel Gibbon's column with information of the result of your examination. The lower part of this creek will be examined by a detachment from Colonel Gibbon's command.

The supply-steamer will be pushed up the Big Horn as far as the forks, if the river is found to be navigable for that distance; and the department commander (who will accompany the column of Colonel Gibbon) desires you to report to him there not later than the expiration of that time for which your troops are rationed, unless in the mean time you receive further orders.

Very respectfully, your obedient servant,

ED. W. SMITH
Captain, Eighteen Infantry, A.A.A.G.
Lieut. Col. G. A. Custer
7th Cavalry.

These were the orders General Terry had given Lieutenant Colonel (brevet Major General) Custer on the 22nd of June. Custer rode off with his regiment. That was the last time General Terry saw of Custer alive.

Report of Lieutenant George D. Wallace, 7th Cavalry.

Saint Paul, Minn., January 27, 1877

Sir: I have the honor to submit the following report of the march and the country passed over by the 7th Regiment of Cavalry from the 22nd to the 25th of June, 1876:

At 12 p.m. on the 22nd of June, 1876, the 7th Cavalry, under Lieutenant-Colonel Custer, left camp on the Yellowstone and moved up that stream for 2 miles to the mouth of the Rosebud, then up the Rosebud. We crossed the latter near its mouth. It was a clear running stream, from 3 to 4 feet wide, and about 3 inches deep; bottom gravel, but in many places water standing in pools. Water slightly alkaline. Owing to delays with the pack-train the command moved only about 12 miles that day. We camped on the left bank of the Rosebud, at the base of a steep bluff. We had plenty of wood and water, and grass for our animals. During the greater part of the march the trail followed the high ground, or second bottom, where the soil was poor, the grass thin, and crowded out by sage-brush and cactus. In the lower part of the valley the soil appeared to be good, the grazing fair, the bottom timbered with large cottonwood. Small willows grew thickly along the banks in many places. For the first 8 miles the hills sloped back gradually, but near camp were more abrupt, and covered with stones and cactus. Several deep ravines were crossed during the day. The only serious obstacle to a wagon-train

would be the numerous crossings of the bends of the Rosebud. Weather clear, but not unpleasantly warm. No game visible. Plenty of fish in the creek.

June 23, 1876. – Orders were given last night that trumpet signals would be discontinued, that the stable-guards would wake their respective companies at 3 a.m., and the command would move at 5 a.m. General Custer stated that short marches would be made for the first few days, after that they would be increased. All were ready at the appointed time, and the command moving out we crossed to the right bank of the Rosebud. The bluff being very broken, we had to follow the valley for some distance, crossing the Rosebud five times in 3 miles; thence up the right side for about 10 miles. There we halted, to allow the pack-train to close up. Soon after starting, crossed to the left bank and followed that for 15 miles, and camped on the right bank at 4:30 p.m., making a distance of over 30 miles. The last of the pack-train did not get into camp until near sunset. About 5 miles from our last camp we came to the trail made by Major Reno, a few days previous, and a few miles further on saw the first traces of the Indian camps. They were all old, but everything indicated a large body of Indians. Every bend of the stream bore traces of some old camp, and their ponies had nipped almost every spear of grass. The ground was strewn with broken bones and cuttings from buffalo hides. The country passed over after the first few miles was rolling, and poor, except along the creek. Grass all eaten up. Plenty of cottonwood along the creek. During the last 5 or 6 miles of the march, the cottonwood timber was gradually replaced by ash and a species of elder. The valley was about one-fourth of a mile wide, and for the last 15 miles the hills were very steep and rocky, sandstone being present. The country back from the hills looked to be very much broken. The hills were covered with a short growth of pines. No game seen during the day; weather warm and clear.

June 24, 1876- The command moved at 5 a.m. this morning. After we had been on the march about an hour, our Crow scouts came in and reported fresh signs of Indians, but in no great numbers. After a short consultation, General Custer, with an escort of two companies, moved out in advance, the remainder of the command following at a distance of about half a mile. We followed the right bank of the Rosebud; crossed two running tributaries, the first we had seen. At 1 p.m. the command was halted, scouts sent ahead, and the men made coffee. The scouts got back about 4, and reported a fresh camp at the forks of the Rosebud. Everything indicated that the Indians were not more than thirty miles away. At 5 p.m. the command moved out; crossed to the left bank of Rosebud; passed through several large camps. The trail now was fresh, and the whole valley scratched up by the trailing lodge-poles. At 7:45 p.m. we encamped on the right bank of Rosebud. Scouts were sent ahead to see which branch of the stream the Indians had followed. Distance marched to-day, about 28 miles. Soil in the valley very good, and in many places grazing very fine. Timber scattering, principally elder and ash. Hills rough and broken, and thickly covered with pines. Weather clear and very warm. About 9 p.m. the scouts returned and reported that the Indians had crossed the divide to the Little Big Horn River. General Custer determined to cross the divide that night (the 24th), to conceal the command, the next day (the 25th) find out the locality of the village, and attack the following morning (the 26th) at daylight. Orders were given to move at midnight, but we did not get off until near 1 a.m., and, owing to delays on account of pack-train, we had only marched about 8 miles when daylight appeared.

We halted, and the men were ordered to make coffee. While waiting here a scout came back from Lieutenant Varnum, who had been sent out the night before. In a note to General Custer, Lieutenant Varnum stated that he could see the smoke of the village about 20 miles away, on the Little Big Horn. The scout pointed out the butte from which the village could be seen. It was about 8 miles ahead.

We moved on, and when near the butte Lieutenant Varnum joined us and reported that the Indians had discovered the command and that he had seen couriers go in the direction of the village. General Custer assembled the officers, told them what he had heard, and said he would move ahead and attack the village without further delay.

At 12 p.m., on the 25th, we crossed the divide between the Rosebud and Little Big Horn. From the divide could be seen the valley of the Little Big Horn, and about 15 or 20 miles to the northwest could be seen a light blue cloud, and to practiced eyes showed that our game was near. A small stream starting from the point near where we crossed the divide flowed in the direction of the smoke. After assignment of battalions was made, General Custer followed down the right bank of the stream, and Major Reno the left. When within three miles of the Little Big Horn, Major Reno was ordered across to the right bank and the two columns moved together for some distance, when Major Reno was ordered ahead. He recrossed this stream, moved down it, crossed the Little Big Horn, halted his command, formed line and moved down the valley and commenced the battle of June 25.

In passing from the Rosebud to the Little Big Horn, we followed up the left branch (current Davis Creek) of the first, then up a dry ravine to the crest of the divide; grass short, soil poor, hills low. From the crest to the Little Big Horn the country was broken and the

valley narrow; some timber along the little stream we followed down. Distance traveled during the night of the 24th and on the 25th about 6 miles.

I am, sir, very respectfully, your obedient servant,

Geo. D. Wallace,
First Lieutenant and Adjutant 7th Cavalry.
The Chief Engineer
Department of Dakota

Five days after General Terry submitted his last orders to General Custer on the 22nd, he submitted the following report to his superior, Lieutenant- General Philip H. Sheridan:

Headquarters Department of Dakota,

Camp on Little Big Horn River, Montana,
June 27, 1876.

To the Adjutant-General of the Military Division of the Missouri,

Chicago, Ill., via Fort Ellis:

It is my painful duty to report that day before yesterday, the 25th instant, a great disaster overtook General Custer and the troops under his command. At 12 o'clock of the 22nd, he started with his whole regiment and a strong detachment of scouts and guides from the mouth of the Rosebud. Proceeding up that river about twenty miles, he struck a very heavy Indian trail which had previously been discovered, and pursuing it, found that it led, as was supposed that it would lead, to the Little Big Horn River. Here he found a village of almost unexampled extent, and at once attacked it with that portion of his force

which was immediately at hand. Major Reno with three companies, A, G, and M, of the regiment, was sent into the valley of the stream, at the point where the trail struck it. General Custer, with five companies, C, E, F, I, and L, attempted to enter it about three miles lower down. Reno forded the river, charged down its left bank, dismounted, and fought on foot until finally, completely overwelmed by numbers, he was compelled to mount, recross the river, and seek a refuge on the high bluffs which overlook its right bank. Just as he recrossed, Captain Benteen, who, with three companies, D, H, and K, was some two miles to the left of Reno when the action commenced, but who had been ordered by General Custer to return, came to the river, and, rightly concluding it was useless for his force to attempt to renew the fight in the valley, he joined Reno on the bluffs. Captain McDougall, with his company, B, was at first some distance in the rear, with the train of pack-mules; he also came up to Reno. Soon this united force was nearly surrounded by Indians, many of whom, armed with rifles of long range, occupied positions which commanded the ground held by the cavalry – ground from which there was no escape. Rifle-pits were dug, and the fight was maintained, though with heavy loss, from about half past two o'clock of the 25th till 6 o'clock of the 26th, when the Indians withdrew from the valley, taking with them their village. Of the movements of General Custer and the five companies under his immediate command scarcely anything is known from those who witnessed them, for no officer or soldier who accompanied him has yet been found alive. His trail, from the point where Reno crossed the stream, passes along and in rear of the rest of the bluffs on the right bank for nearly three miles. Then it comes down on the bank of the river, but at once diverges from it as if he had unsuccessfully attempted to cross;then turns upon itself, almost completes a circle, and ceases. It is marked by the remains of his officers and men and the bodies of his horses, some of them dotted along the path, others heaped in ravines and upon knolls, where halts appear to have been made. There is abundant evidence that a gallant resistance was offered by the troops, but that they were beset on all sides by overpowering numbers. The officers known to be killed are: General Custer, Captains Keogh, Yates, and Custer, Lieutenants Cook, Smith, McIntosh, Calhoun, Porter, Hodgson, Sturgis, and Riley, of the cavalry; Lieutenant Crittenden, of the Twentieth Infantry; and Acting Assistant Surgeon DeWolf. Lieutenant Harrington, of the calvary, and Assistant Surgeon Lord are missing; Captain Benteen and Lieutenant Varnum, of the cavalry, are slightly wounded. Mr. Boston Custer, a brother, and Mr. Reed, a nephew, of General Custer, were both with him and were killed. No other officers than those whom I have named are among the killed, wounded, and missing.

*It is impossible as yet to obtain a nominal list of the enlisted men who were killed and wounded; but the number of killed, including officers, must reach 250; the number wounded is 51. At the mouth of the Rosebud, I informed General Custer that I should take the supply-steamer "*Far West*" up the Yellowstone to ferry General Gibbon's column over the river; that I should personally accompany that column; and that it would, in all probability, reach the mouth of the Little Big Horn on the 26th instant. The steamer reached General Gibbon's troops, near the mouth of the Big Horn, early in the morning of the 24th, and at 4 o'clock in the afternoon all his men and animals were across the Yellowstone. At 5 o'clock, the column, consisting of five companies of the 7th Infantry, four companies of the Second Cavalry, and a battery of three Gatling guns, marched out to and across Tullock's*

Creek. Starting soon after 5 o'clock in the morning of the 25th, the infantry made a march of twenty-two miles over the most difficult county which I have ever seen. In order that scouts might be sent into the valley of the Little Big Horn, the cavalry, with the battery, was then pushed on thirteen or fourteen miles further, reaching camp at midnight. The scouts were sent out at half past 4 in the morning of the 26th. They soon discovered three Indians, who at first were supposed to be Sioux; but, when overtaken they proved to be Crows, who had been with General Custer. They brought the first intelligence of the battle. Their story was not credited. It was supposed that some fighting, perhaps severe fighting, had taken place; but it was not believed that disaster could have overtaken so large a force as twelve companies of cavalry. The infantry, which had broken camp very early, soon came up, and the whole column entered and moved up the valley of the Little Big Horn. During the afternoon efforts were made to send scouts through to what was supposed to be General Custer's position, to obtain information of the condition of affairs; but those who were sent out were driven back by parties of Indians, who, in increasing numbers, were seen hovering in General Gibbon's front. At twenty minutes before 9 o'clock in the evening, the infantry had marched between twenty-nine and thirty miles. The men were very weary and daylight was fading. The column was therefore halted for the night, at a point about eleven miles in a straight line above the mouth of the stream. This morning the movement was resumed, and, after a march of nine miles, Major Reno's intrenched position was reached. The withdrawal of the Indians from around Reno's command and from the valley was undoubtedly caused by the approach of General Gibbon's troops. Major Reno and Captain Benteen, both of whom are officers of

great experience, accustomed to see large masses of mounted men, estimate the number of Indians engaged at not less than twenty-five hundred. Other officers think that the number was greater than this. The village in the valley was about three miles in length and about a mile in width. Besides the lodges proper, a great number of temporary brush-wood shelters was found in it, indicating that many men besides its proper inhabitants had gathered together there. Major Reno is very confident that there were a number of white men fighting with the Indians. It is believed that the loss of the Indians was large. I have as yet received no official reports in regard to the battle; but what is stated herein is gathered from the officers who were on the ground then and from those who have been over it since.

ALFRED H. TERRY
Bridadier-General.

Headquarters Department of Dakota.

Camp on Little Horn, June 28, 1876.

Assistant Adjutant-General,

Military Division of the Missouri, Chicago, Ill.:

The wounded were brought down from the bluffs last night and made as comfortable as our means would permit. To-day horse and hand litters have been constructed, and this evening we shall commence moving the wounded toward the mouth of the Little Big Horn, to which point I hope the steamer has been able to come. The removal will occupy three or four days, as the marches must be short.

> ***A reconnaissance was made today by Captain Ball, of the Second Cavalry, along the trail made by the Indians when they left the valley. He reports that they divided into two parties, one of which kept to the valley of the Long Fork, making, he thinks, for the Big Horn Mountains; the other turned more to the eastward. He also discovered a very heavy trail leading into the valley that is not more than five days old. This trail is entirely distinct from the one which Custer follwed, and would seem to show that at least two large bands united here just before the battle. The dead were all buried to-day.***
>
> ***ALFRED H. TERRY,***
> ***Brigadier-General.***

On the 28th, before he left the battlefield heading north with the wounded, General Terry ordered Lieutenant Edward Maguire, chief engineer assigned to the expedition, to make a detailed survey and report of the battlefield. Lieutenant Maguire's map was to become the key reference piece two and one half years later during the Reno Court of Inquiry. The ford which Major Reno and his column made at the south end of the valley was designated Ford A. The skirmish line his force made while in the valley was designated C. The ford at the Medicine Tail Coulee and Little Bighorn River would become infamously known as Ford B. The positions of the dead found on the hillside were designated reference points such as H for a Deep Ravine in which twenty-eight dead of Company E were found, and E where General Custer and a number of officers were found along with the dead of Company F, and designation D, where the dead of Company L and nearby Company I lay dead. This report began the long debate on how the battle might have been fought. It was filed on July 10, 1876.

ANNUAL REPORT OF LIEUTENANT EDWARD MAGUIRE,

CORPS OF ENGINEERS, FOR THE FISCAL YEAR ENDING JUNE 30, 1876.

EXPLORATIONS AND SURVEYS IN THE DEPARTMENT OF DAKOTA.

CAMP ON THE YELLOWSTONE RIVER,

NEAR THE MOUTH OF THE BIG HORN RIVER,

July 10, 1876.

GENERAL: I have the honor to submit the following report of operations in the Department of Dakota from the date of my assignment to duty as chief engineer of the department to the close of the fiscal year ending June 30, 1876.

In obedience to orders received from the Adjutant-General's Office, I reported in person to Brig. Gen. A. H. Terry, at St. Paul, Minn., on the evening of May 8, and was assigned to duty vice Capt. Wm. Ludlow, Corps of Engineers, United States Army, relieved. In compliance with orders from headquarters Department of Dakota, I left Saint Paul early on the morning of the 10th, and proceeded to Fort Lincoln, Dakota Territory, to join the troops about to take the field against the hostile Sioux. Mr. W. H. Wood, assistant engineer, with the detachment of enlisted men, had preceded me some days. On arriving at Fort Lincoln, I learned from the commanding general that, unless the services of my assistant were necessary, it was desirable that he should not accompany the column. As his services would have been simply a convenience to me, and in no respect a necessity, I directed him to return to Saint Paul, where he has remained. The detachment of the battalion of engineers, consisting

of Sergeant Wilson and Privates Goslin and Culligan, has accompanied me on the expedition, and has performed most excellent service. Sergeant Becker, with two privates, had, previous to my assignment, been ordered to Montana to acompany the column under command of Colonel Gibbon, 7th Infantry.

After a detention of a few days near Fort Lincoln, due to rain, we finally broke camp at 5 a.m., May 17, and the march westward was commenced. The column was commanded by Brig. Gen. A. H. Terry, and was composed of the following troops: The 7th Cavalry, commanded by Lieut. Col. G. A. Custer; a battalion of infantry, commanded by Capt. L. H. Sanger, Seventeenth Infantry; headquarters' guard, consisting of one company of the Sixth Infantry, commanded by Capt. Stephen Baker; a battery of three ½ inch Gatling guns, commanded by Second Lieut. W. H. Low, Twentieth Infantry; 45 Indian scouts, guides, and interpreters, under the command of Second Lieut. C. A. Varnum, 7th Cavalry; the wagon and pack-trains and herd, with their numerous attaches. There was a total of 50 officers, 968 enlisted men, 190 civilian employees, and 1,694 animals.

I was furnished with a four-mule ambulance for the transportation of my instruments and men. To the wheels of this ambulance were attached the odometers.

The column reached Powder River without having seen an Indian, nor even a trace of recent origin. The only difficulties encountered, with the exception of a snow-storm, which commenced the night of the 31st of May and lasted until the 3d of June, were those offered by nature of the country to the passage of a heavily-loaded train. There was not a day that bridging was not necessary; but the journey through Davis Creek to the Little Missouri, through the Bad Lands immediately west of the latter stream, and then the descent

into the valley of the Powder, demanded almost incessant bridging and road-making. We reached Powder River late in the evening of June 7. From this camp, Major Reno, 7th Cavalry, with six companies of his regiment, was sent on a scout up Powder River to the forks, thence across to the Rosebud, and back to the mouth of the Tongue. On June 11, we marched down the valley of the Powder, and reached the Yellowstone, where a depot was established under command of Major Moore, Sixth Infantry. Leaving the wagon-train at this point, Lieutenant Colonel Custer, with the troops and pack-train, proceeded to the mouth of the Tongue River. General Terry and staff went on the steamboat to the same place, there meeting Major Reno, who reported that he had found a fresh heavy Indian trail, leaving the Rosebud in a westerly direction. The whole command was then moved up the Yellowstone to the mouth of the Rosebud, where we met Gibbon's column. At this point, a definite plan of campaign was decided upon; and, as this plan clearly set forth in the letter of instruction furnished to Custer, I insert it in full:

(Author's note: see the previously mentioned June 22 orders from General Terry to Custer, as they are here referenced by Lieutenant Maguire in his report)

These instructions were supplemented by verbal information to Custer, that he could expect to find Gibbon's column at the mouth of the Little Big Horn not later than the 26th.

Pursuant to these instructions, Custer took up his line of march about noon on the 22d of June. His command (counting officers, enlisted men, and civilians) numbered nearly 650 mounted men. Both man and beast were in excellent condition, and there was not one of the command who was not filled with high hopes of success. Upon Custer's departure, General

Terry and staff proceeded up the Yellowstone with Gibbon's column, and when near the mouth of the Big Horn the command was crossed to the right bank of the former stream. Gibbon's column, as now constituted, consisted of four companies of the Second Cavalry, five companies of the 7th Infantry, and Lieutenant Low's Gatling Battery, amounting in all (including the civilian employees) to 377 fighting men. The night of June 24, we passed in camp on Tulloch's Creek. The next day we crossed the divide between Tulloch's Creek, and the Big Horn, and reached the latter stream after a severe march of twenty-two miles. The country was exceedingly rough, hill after hill and ravine after ravine, but with little grass and plenty of the ubiquitous sage and cactus. The soil was alkaline, and the air was filled with dust, clogging up the nostrils, ears, and throat. In addition to this, the day was very warm, and not a drop of water to be obtained on the march. The infantry had understood that we were to follow Tulloch's Creek, and knowing that in that case they could obtain water at any time they did not fill their canteens. The consequence was that they sufferd terribly, and numbers of men toward the close of the march dropped on the way, utterly exhausted. The refreshing sight of the Big Horn finally gladdened their hearts, and those on the road having been brought in, they remained in camp that night. General Terry, taking the cavalry, pushed on, and a most wearisome and disheartening march we made of it. The night was black, and a cold rain drenched us. Besides this, we were obliged to cross a very rough country; and the descent and ascent of steep declivities, with no other guide than the occasional white horse, (if so lucky as to get directly behind one,) was anything but pleasant. The Indian scouts finally found a pool of alkaline water after a march of 12 miles, and we encamped in the mud for the short remaining portion

of the night. About 11 o'clock the following morning (June 26) we were joined by the infantry near the mouth of the Little Big Horn, and we then proceeded up the valley of that river. We went into camp that night only after the infantry had made a march of more than 50 miles in two days. The next morning the march was resumed, and we sighted two teepees in the valley. These teepees were filled with dead warriors, and were all that remained standing of a large Indian village. We found the ground strewn with skins, robes, camp-equipage, &c. indicating that the village had been hastily removed. The cavalry-saddles and dead horses lying around gave us the first inkling of the fact that there had been a fight, and that the troops had been worsted; but we were not prepared for the whole truth. As we passed on, we were met by Lieutenant Wallace, of the 7th Cavalry, who informed us that Major Reno, with the remnant of seven companies, was intrenched on the bluffs across the river, where he had sustained a siege for nearly two days desperations. We ascended the steep bluffs, and the welcome we received was such as to move even the most callous. Officers and men relieved their surcharged natures by hysterical shouts and tears. The question then arose on all sides, "Where is Custer?" The reply came only too soon. About 3 miles below Reno's position, we found the hills covered with the dead bodies of officers and men.

Of Custer's fight we at present know nothing, and can only surmise. We must be content with the knowledge gleaned from the appearance of the field, that they died as only brave men can die, and that this battle, slaughter as it was, was fought with the gallantry and desperation of which the "Charge of the Light Brigade" cannot boast. The bodies, with but few exceptions, were frightfully mutilated, and horrors stared us in the face at every step.

I proceed to give the details of Custer's march from the Rosebud, and of the battle, as I have been able to collect them up at the present time. On the 22d they marched 12 miles; on the 23d they marched 35 miles; on the 24th they marched from 5 a.m. till 8 p.m., or about 45 miles; they then rested for four hours. At 12 they started again and proceeded 10 miles. They were then about 23 miles from the village. They reached the village about 2 p.m. on the 25th. They had made a march of 78 miles in a day and a half, and, Captain Benteen tells me, without a drop of water. At some distance from the village, Custer made his disposition of the regiment. He ordered Benteen, with three companies, to move to the left and scour the country for Indians. He ordered Reno, with three companies, to advance parallel with his (Custer's) own command. When the village was sighted, he ordered Reno to charge with his three companies, telling him that he would be supported. Reno crossed the river at the point A, (see sketch herewith,) and moved down the woods at C without encountering much opposition. On reaching the latter point, the men were dismounted and deployed as skirmishers on the line indicated on the sketch. The Indians immediately swarmed around them, and Reno, finding that they were getting in his rear in large numbers, remounted his command and charged through them in retreat to the bluffs on the opposite side of the river. There were Indians on all sides of them, and Lieutenant McIntosh and several enlisted men were actually pulled from their horses and butchered. The command, with some loss, including Lieutenant Hodgson, reached the bluffs, and, being joined by Benteen and his command, they succeeded in keeping the Indians off. Benteen had received an order from Custer to hurry up, as the village had been struck, and in moving up he saw Reno's retreat, and joined him on the bluffs

as quickly as possible. The Indians were all around them, and kept an incessant fire of unerring accuracy. In the mean time, Custer had gone down stream and attempted to make a crossing at the point B, but was met by an overpowering force, as the troops retreated to the hills in rear in order to procure a more defensible position. From the position of the dead bodies on the field, I conclude that they retreated on the two lines marked on the sketch to concentrate at E, which was the highest point of the ground. At the hill D a stand was undoubtedly made by the company under command of Lieutenant Calhoun to protect the men passing up to E. Lieutenants Calhoun and Critenden were killed on this hill. Captain Keogh was killed about half-way up the slope to E. The column which retreated along the line B H E must have been dismounted, and, fighting along the whole distance, a portion of the men taking to the ravine H for shelter, must have been surrounded by the Indians. There were twenty-eight bodies found in this ravine. From H to E stretched a line of dead men with skirmish intervals. The crest E was litterally covered with dead officers and men. Here we found General Custer and his brother, Captain Custer, Captain Yates, Lieutenant Smith, Lieutenant Cook, and Lieutenant Riley. The Indians must have been present in overwelming numbers, for this part of the fight did not, from all accounts, last over two or three hours.

As night came on, the attack on Reno ceased, and the troops were enabled to intrench. The attack was renewed early on the morning of the 26th, and continued until late in the afternoon, when the Indians, seeing Gibbon's column advancing in the distance left Reno, and, packing up their village, moved off toward the Big Horn Mountains. The number of Indians is estimated to have been 3,000 warriors, and they marched off with all the precision of movement and regularity of formation of the best drilled soldiers. The officers tell me that they were well drilled and disciplined. Volleys were fired by them at the commands "Ready! Aim!! Fire!!!"

The casualties of the 7th Cavalry are as follows:

Killed.- Lieut. Col. G. A. Custer, 7th Cavalry; Capt. M. W. Keogh, 7th Cavalry; Capt. G. W. Yates, 7th Cavalry; Capt. T. W. Custer, 7th Cavalry; Lieutenant W. W. Cook, 7th Cavalry; Lieut. A. E. Smith, 7th Cavalry; Lieut. McIntosh, 7th Cavalry; Lieut. J. Calhoun, 7th Cavalry; Lieut. J. E. Porter, 7th Cavalry; Lieut. B. H. Hodgson, 7th Cavalry; Lieut. H. M. Harrington, 7th Cavalry; Lieut. J. C. Sturgis, 7th Cavalry; Lieut. W. V. W. Riley, 7th Cavalry; Asst. Surg. G. E. Lord; Act. Asst. Surg. DeWolf; Lieut. J. J. Crittenden, Twentieth Infantry – 16 officers; 252 enlisted men; 9 civilian employes; 277 killed; 59 wounded. The number of Indians killed and wounded is not known.

We remained two days on the field to bury the dead and burn the material left by the Indians, and then returned to the boat with the wounded, who have all been sent to Fort Lincoln. We are here waiting in camp for instructions.

There are some conclusions which force themselves upon the mind as indubitable. They are as follows:

1st. The number of Indians was underestimated at the outset of the campaign.

2d. The courage, skill, and, in short, the general fighting ability of the Indians has heretofore been underestimated and scoffed at. It has been forgotten that the Indian traders, by furnishing the Indians with the best breech-loading arms, and all the ammunition they desire, have totally changed the problem of Indian warfare. Sitting Bull has displayed the best generalship in this campaign. He has kept his troops well in hand, and, moving on interior lines, he has beaten us in detail.

3d. The Indians are the best irregular cavalry in the world, and are superior in horsemanship and marksmanship to our soldiers, besides being better armed. Our regiments of cavalry are composed of men about three-fourths of whom are recruits, who have never fought with Indians. They never drilled at firing on horseback, and the consequence is that the horses are as unused to fighting as the men themselves, and become unruly in action.

4th. The carbine has not a significiently long effective range, and, considering it simply as a weapon for close encounters, it has not the advantages of a magazine-gun.

The trail has been kept, and observations with the sextant have been made whenever practicable.

Very respectfully, your obedient servant,
EDW. MAGUIRE
First Lieutenant Corps of Engineers,
Chief Engineer, Department of Dakota,

Big. Gen. A. A. Humphreys,
Chief of Engineers, U. S. A.

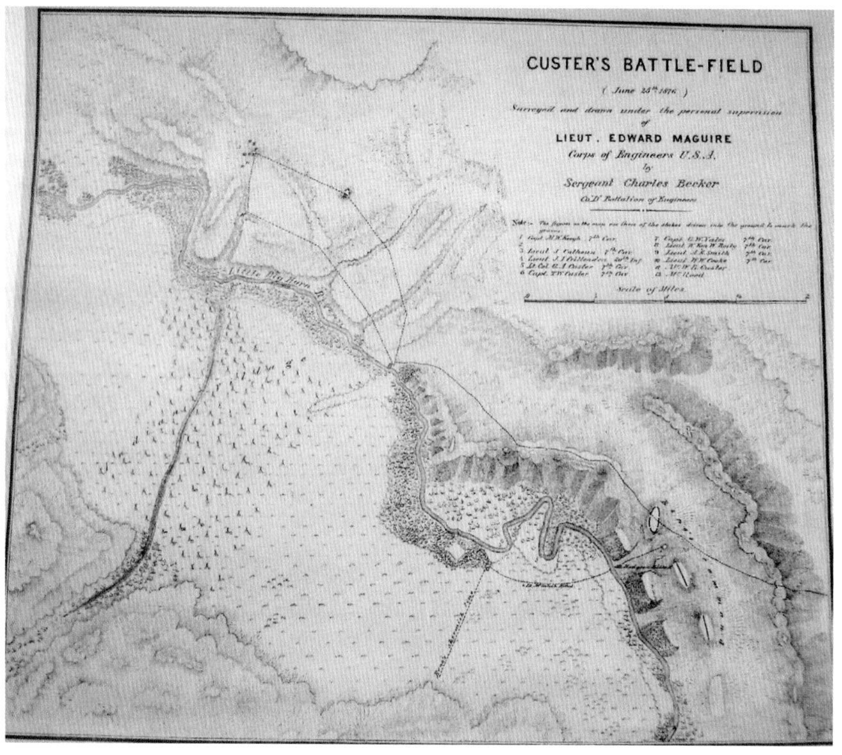
CUSTER'S BATTLE-FIELD
(June 25th 1876)
Surveyed and drawn under the personal supervision
of
LIEUT. EDWARD MAGUIRE
Corps of Engineers U.S.A.
by
Sergeant Charles Becker
Scale of Miles

As the reports were being prepared and sent to military higher-ups, the press began to receive information on the battle as well. The *Bismark Tribune* had managed to have a reporter, Mark Kellogg, assigned to the expedition. He had furnished reports to the *Bismark Tribune*-on the progress of the column, which had originated at Fort Lincoln. Mr. Kellogg's last report was never published or found. He had ridden with Custer that fateful day and died with his observations. On July 6, 1876 the *Bismark Tribune* ran a "Tribune Extra," it read as follows:

First Account of the Custer Massacre

Massacred . . . Gen. Custer And 261 Men The Victims

No Officer or Man of 5 Companies Left To Tell The Tale.

3 days Desperate Fighting by Maj. Reno and the Remainder of the 7th.

Full Details of the Battle.

List of Killed and Wounded.

The* Bismark Tribune's *Special Correspondent Slain.

Squaws Mutilate and Rob the Dead.

Victims Captured Alive Tortured in a Most Fiendish Manner.

What Will Congress Do About It?

Shall This Be the Beginning of The End?

It will be remembered that the Bismark Tribune *sent a special correspondent with Gen. Terry, who was the only professional correspondent with the expedition. Kellogg's last words to the writer: "We leave the Rosebud tomorrow and by the time this reaches you we will have met and (punished) the red devils, with what results remain to be seen. I go with Custer and will be at the death." How true. On the morning of the 22d Gen. Custer took up the line of march for the trail of the Indians, reported by Reno on the Rosebud. Gen. Terry apprehending danger, urged Custer to take additional men but Custer, having full confidence in his men and their ability to cope with the Indians in whatever force he might meet them, declined the proffered assistance and marched with his regiment alone. He was instructed to strike the trail of the Indians, to follow it until he discovered their position and report by courier to Gen. Terry who would reach the mouth of Little Horn by evening of the 26th. Custer scouts reported the location of the village recently deserted, whereupon Custer went in to camp, marching again at 11 p.m. continuing the march until daylight, when he again went into camp for coffee. Custer was then fifteen miles from the village located on the Little Horn, one of the branches of the Big Horn, twenty miles above its mouth.*

General Custer pushed on. The Indians by this time had discovered his approach and soon were seen mounting in great haste, riding here and there. It was presumed in full retreat. This idea was strengthened by finding a freshly abandoned Indian camp with a deserted teepee, in which one of their dead had been left, about six miles from where the battle took place. Custer with his usual vigor pushed on making seventy-eight miles without sleep and attacked the village near its foot with companies C, E, F, L, and I, of the 7th Cavalry, Reno having in the mean time attacked at its head with three companies of cavalry which being surrounded, after a desperate hand-to-hand conflict, in which many were killed and wounded, cut their way to a bluff about three hundred feet high, where they were reinforced by four companies of cavalry under Col. Benteen. In gaining this position Col. Reno had to recross the Little Horn, and at the ford the hottest fight occurred. It was here where Lieutenants McIntosh, Hodgson and Dr. Wolf fell; where Charley Reynolds fell in a hand-to-hand conflict with a dozen or more Sioux emptying several chambers of his revolver, each time bringing a red skin before he was brought down – shot through the heart. It was here Bloody Knife surrendered his spirit to the one who gave it righting the natural and hereditary foes of his rifle as well as the foes of the whites.

The Sioux dashed up beside the soldiers in some instances knocking them from their horses and killing them at the pleasure of the red devils. This was the case with Lt. McIntosh, who was unarmed swept with a saber. He was pulled from his horse, tortured and finally murdered at the pleasure of the red devils. It was here that (scout Fred) Girard was separated from the command and lay all night with the wrenching floods dealing death and destruction to his comrades within a few feet of him, and, but time will not permit me to relate the story, through some means succeeded in saving his fine black stallion in which he took so much pride. The ford was crossed and the summit of the bluffs, having, Col. Smith says, the steepest sides that he ever saw ascended by a horse or mule reached through, the ascent was made under a galling fire.

The companies engaged in this affair were those of Captain (M)oylan, French and McIntosh. Col. Reno had gone ahead with three companies in obedience to the order of Gen. Custer, fighting most gallantly, driving back repeatedly the Indians who charged in their front, but the fire from the bluff being so galling, forced the movement heretofore alluded to. Signals were given and

soon Benteen with the four companies in reserve came up in time to save Reno from the fate with which Custer about this time met. The Indians charged the hill time and again but were each time reprised with heavy slaughter of its gallant defenders. Soon, however, they reached bluffs higher than those occupied by Reno and opened a destructive fire from points beyond the reach of cavalry carbines. Nothing being heard from Custer, Col. Weir was ordered to push his command along the bank of the river in the direction he was supposed to be, but he was soon driven back, retiring with difficulty. About this time the Indians received strong reinforcements and litterally swarmed the hill sides and on the plains, coming so near at times that stones were thrown into the ranks of Col. Reno's command by those unarmed or out of ammunition. Charge after charge in quick succession, the fight being sometimes almost hand to hand. But they drew off finally, taking to the hills and ravines. Col. Benteen charged a large party in a ravine, driving them from it in confusion. They evidently trusted in their numbers and did not look for so bold a movement. They were within range of the corral and wounded several packers. J. C. Wagoner, among the number, in the head, while many horses and mules were killed. Near 10 o'clock the fight closed, and the men worked all night strengthening their breastworks, using knives, tin cups and plates, in place of spades and picks, taking up the fight again in the morning. In the afternoon of the second day the desire for water became almost intolerable. The wounded were begging piteously for it; the tongues of the men were swollen and their lips parched and from the lack of rest they were almost exhausted. So a bold attempt was made for water. Men volunteered to go with canteens and camp kettles, though to go was almost certain death. The attempt succeeded though in making it one man was killed and several wounded. The men were relieved, and that night the animals were watered. The fight closed at

dark, opening again next morning and continuing until the afternoon of the 27th. Meantime the men became more and more exhausted and all wondered what had happened to Custer. A panic all at once was created among the Indians and they stampeded from the hills and from the valleys and the village was soon deserted except for the dead. Reno and his brave hand felt that succor was nigh. Gen. Terry came in sight, and strong men wept upon each others necks, but no word was had from Custer. Handshaking and congratulations were scarcely over when Lt. Bradley reported he had found Custer dead, with one hundred and ninety cavalry men. Imagine the effect. Words cannot picture the feeling of these, his comrades and soldiers. Gen. Terry sought the site and found it to be true. Of those brave men who followed Custer, all perished; no one lives to tell his story of the battle. Those deployed as skimishers, lay as they fell, shot down from every side having been entirely surrounded in an open plain. The men in the companies fell in platoons, and like those on the skirmish line, lay as they fell, with their officers behind them in proper positions. General Custer, who was shot through the head and body, seemed to have been among the last to fall and around him lay the bodies of Col. Tom and Boston, his brothers, Col. Calhoun; his brother-in-law, and his nephew young Reed who insisted on accompanying the expedition for pleasure. Col. Cook and the members of he non-commissioned staff all dead – all stripped of their clothing and many of them with bodies terribly mutilated. The squaws seem to have passed over the field and crushed the skulls of the wounded and dying with stones and clubs. The hands of some were severed from the body, the privates of some were cut off, while others bore traces of torture, arrows having been shot into their private parts while yet living or other means of torture adopted. The officers who fell were as follows; Gen. G. A. Custer; Cols. Geo. Yates, Miles Keogh, James Calhoun,

W. W. Cook, Capts. McIntosh, A. E. Smith, Lieutenants Riley, Critenden, Sturgis, Harrington, Hodgson and Porter. Asst. Surgeon DeWolf. The only citizens killed were Boston Custer, Mr. Reed, Charles Reynolds, Isaiah, the interpreter from Fort Rice and Mark Kellogg, the latter the Tribune correspondent. The body of Kellogg alone remained unstripped of its clothing and was not mutilated. Perhaps as they had learned to respect the Great Chief Custer, and for that reason did not mutilate his remains they had in like manner learned to respect this humble shover of the lead pencil and to that fact may be attributed this result. The wounded were sent to the rear some fourteen miles on horse litters striking the Far West sixty odd miles up the Big Horn which point they left on Monday at noon reaching Bismark nine hundred miles distant at 10 p.m.

The burial of the dead was sad work but they were all decently interred. Many could not be recognized; among the latter class were some of the officers. This work being done the command wended its way back to the base where Gen. Terry awaits supplies and approval of his plans for the future campaign.

The men are worn out with marching and fighting and are almost wholly destitute of clothing.

The Indians numbered at least eighteen hundred lodges in their permanent camp, while those who fought Crook seems to have joined them, making their effective fighting force nearly four thousand. These were led by chiefs carrying flags of various colors, nine of which were found in a burial tent on the field of battle. Many other dead were found on the field, and near it ten squaws at one point in the ravine– evidently the work of Ree or Crow scouts.

The Indian dead were in great number, as they were constantly assaulting an inferior force. The camp had the appearance being abandoned in haste. The most gorgeous ornaments were found on the bodies of the dead chiefs, and hundreds of finely dressed and painted robes and skins were thrown about the camp. The Indians were certainly severely punished.

We said of those who went in battle with Custer none are living– one Crow scout himself in the field, and witnessed and survived the battle. His story is plausible, and is accepted, but we have not room for it now . . .

The total number killed was two hundred and sixty one, wounded 52. Thirty-eight of the wounded were brought down on the Far West; three of them died en route. The remainder are cared for at the field hospital.

DeRudio had a narrow escape and his escape is attributed in the noise of beavers, jumping into the river during the engagement. DeRudio followed them, got out of sight, and after hiding for twelve hours or more finally reached the command in safety.

The body of Lt. Hodgson did not fall into the hands of the Indians, that of Lt. McIntosh did and was badly mutilated; McIntosh, although a half-breed was a gentleman of culture and esteemed by all who knew him. He leaves a family at Lincoln, as does Gen. Custer, Cols. Calhoun, Yates, Capt. Smith and Lt. Porter. The unhappy Mrs. Calhoun loses a husband, three brothers and a nephew. Lt. Harrington also had a family, but no trace of his remains was found . . ."

2

Events Leading Up to the Battle

History is a continuation of events from prior times. Such was the Battle of the Little Bighorn. Much of the beginnings of the historical momentum for the Little Bighorn battle began in the year 1862, fourteen years prior. The United States was engaged in the Civil War. The Army of the United States was being tested, defeated many times, by the armies of the Confederacy. With each defeat, President Lincoln would promote new generals, new leaders. His hope was to find strong leaders who would bring victory. In the East, General George McClellan was put in charge. In the West, General Grant was finding victory, first at Fort Donelson, and then at Shiloh, in Tennessee.

Captain George Custer rode with the cavalry. He had the eye of General McClellan upon him. General McClellan had failed in his Peninsular Campaign in Virginia in spring of that year. But so too, Major General John Pope had failed at the Second Battle of Bull Run. Pope was transferred to the frontier state of Minnesota. McClellan was put back in charge of the Army of the Potomic to stop General Robert E. Lee at Sharpsburg, Maryland, on the Antietam Creek.

McClellan's troops managed to stop Lee's invasion of Maryland. However, he failed to crush Lee's defeated armies before they escaped over the Potomic River into Virginia.

President Lincoln went to Sharpsburg to review and scold General McClellan for his failure. In a picture of Lincoln and McClellan in camp, off to the side stands a lone captain, Captain George Custer.

In Congress, it was seen that the railroads of the time were proving to be a strategic and tactical necessity. The railroads would move armies to meet the crises of the battlefield, both North and South. California and its resources on the Pacific were separated from the rest of the Union by the great open spaces of the Indian Territories of the West. Hence, the Pacific Railway Act of 1862 was passed. This act granted large land grants to the railroads to further a transcontinental railroad system to connect the far lands of the West with the East.

In 1862, the construction of the St. Paul and Pacific Railroad was begun. This would later become a part of the railroad empire of James J. Hill and his Great Northern Railroad. In 1864, the Northern Pacific Railroad was chartered by Congress to run from Duluth, Minnesota to Puget Sound in the Washington Territory. Large tracts of land in the Dakota and Montana territories were given to the railroads for purposes of laying track. These tracts were also for giving land to new immigrant settlers to encourage development of the land around the railroads. The railroads would advertise in European newspapers of the opportunities for settlement in America with free land offerings.

With the nation focused on the great battles of the Civil War in the East, troubles were brewing in the state of Minnesota. In 1851 a treaty with the Wahpeton and Sisseton Sioux had been signed. This treaty ceded much of the western lands of current Minnesota, and a portion of lands in Iowa and the Dakotas to the United States. By 1854, white settlers were pushing the Sioux onto small reservations along the Minnesota River. In the spring of 1857, Inkpaduta (Scarlet Point), an outlawed Wahpekute Sioux chief, and a small band of renegade warriors raided and murdered thirty people at Lake Okoboji, Iowa, in the Spirit Lake Massacre.

They then went to Jackson County in western Minnesota and killed several more people. The United States government put pressure on Chief Little Crow of the reservation Sioux in Minnesota to apprehend Inkpaduta. Inkpaduta escaped to the Dakota Territory to the west.

The Sioux of Little Crow's Mdewakanton tribe failed to apprehend Inkpaduta. In addition, monies for Indian agencies from Washington were delayed due to the war. Annuities for provisions and supplies for the reservation were not paid. Growing hunger put pressure on the Indians to satisfy tribal needs. As the German immigrant population in the area grew, new pressures were confronting the reservation Indians. Land was developed for agriculture near the reservations. Traditional hunting grounds, which fed the Indians, were being cleared and planted by the new Minnesota citizens and immigrants.

On August 17, 1862, at Acton, Minnesota, on the farm of Howard Baker, tensions finally flared into violence. The Baker family was killed by a small group of Indians: Brown Wing, Breaking Up, Killing Ghost, and Runs Against Something Crawling. Originally they were stealing eggs from Baker's mother's farm not far away. As the Indians' anger about the whites grew, a courage challenge was made by one of them. They then killed the Bakers and four others.

Tensions grew on the Minnesota reservations as the Indians debated going to war with the whites to protect the four warriors. As described in the book, *The Dakota War of 1862: Minnesota's Other Civil War,* Chief Little Crow knew the whites were as plentiful as "locusts," yet agreed to make war on the whites of the Minnesota River Valley. A bloody war began. Several sharp battles occurred in August and September of that year. President Lincoln and the War Department reassigned General John Pope to head a newly created Military District of the Northwest, with headquarters in St. Paul. General Henry Sibley, Minnesota's first state governor, led his 3000 troops in decisive battles against the Sioux, which ended the major actions of the war. The hostilities in

Minnesota ended in October 1862. Approximately five hundred whites had been killed. The Sioux tribes were either on the run in Dakota, confined to the Minnesota reservations, or temporarily relocated to Mankato, Minnesota. Here 303 warriors stood trial, awaiting death by hanging. President Lincoln personally pardoned all but thirty-nine. On December 26, 1862, thirty-eight Sioux were hung together on the gallows. Indian survivors still in Mankato were force-marched to Fort Snelling on the banks of the Minnesota and Mississippi rivers. They had to endure disease, hunger, and a harsh Minnesota winter in an internment camp on the riverflats below the fort.

The white settlers were not satisfied with the justice meted out. In 1863, General Pope sent expeditions into the Dakota Territory to hunt down the Indians who had escaped west. Military expeditions continued to hunt down those Indians not captured or interned. Operations against the Sioux continued under General Alfred Sully throughout 1864 and into the late 1860s.

In the meantime, the great battles of the Civil War continued. General Ulysses Grant with his friend and subordinate, General William Tecumseh Sherman, were defeating the Confederate armies in Tennesee and at Vicksburg, Mississippi. Out East, the great battle at Gettysburg was deciding the fate of the war and of careers. General Robert E. Lee made a last desperate attempt on July 3, 1863, to break the Union Army. He sent General George Pickett's division and two other divisions on a fateful charge against the Union center on Cemetery Ridge. Confronting him was the Union Second Corps under Major General Winfield Scott Hancock. The brunt of the attack would be met by Brigadier General John Gibbon's Second Division, including the remnants of the famous First Minnesota Regiment.

To assist this grand assault, General Lee had dispatched General Jeb Stuart and his Confederate cavalry to circle around the Union right. This was to divert Union forces away from the main attack. But, quite possibly, this movement, if successful, was to continue and meet the forces of Pickett on the top of Cemetery Ridge, completing a total Confederate victory. As the battle evolved, Stuart's cavalry encountered the Union cavalry. Stuart's men were close to routing the Union cavalrymen. Then out of the woods and onto the field came the cavalry brigade of the Michigan Wolverines, led by George Armstrong Custer. Leading from the front with saber raised, Custer and his cavarlymen defeated the Confederate cavalry.

General Gibbon and his men on Cemetery Ridge tore into the brunt of Pickett's division. The First Minnesota Regiment had suffered grievously the day before in a sacrificial charge ordered by General Hancock to stop an Alabama brigade. Of the 262 men who charged on July 2nd, forty-seven were standing and available for duty after that charge. On July 3rd, the few survivors of the First Minnesota, and the Second Corps of General Hancock took on Pickett's Virginians. Pickett's Charge would be the high- water mark of the Confederacy. The Confederates would lose, but the careers of generals were being won with honors.

By 1864, Grant had assumed total command of the Union armies. His friend General Sherman was burning Atlanta and marching through Georgia to the sea. General Grant's other trusted subordinate, General Philip Sheridan, was clearing out the Shenandoah Valley of Virginia, using a brutal "total war" concept. He burned and destroyed anything of use to the Confederates. Sheridan led a rallying charge after Union troops had been routed at Winchester, Virginia. The "Little General" became a press favorite and a favorite of General Grant. With subordinates including George Custer, he cleared out this part of Virginia.

When Grant planned to trap Lee's armies in 1865 around Richmond and Petersburg, he called upon Sheridan to command his westernmost forces. Sheridan, in turn, ordered Custer to lead the final chase and confrontation at Appomattox. Grant commended Sheridan. Sheridan commended Custer. Grant, the general in the private's coat, did not especially appreciate the flashy and popular Custer. After all, Custer had been a McClellan man.

With the end of the Civil War, a different war began for the War Department. First, there was the war for commands within the Army. There were too many generals and too few troops to command. In the West, renegade Indians attacking settlers and railroad survey crews required military protection and action by the Army. As Grant addressed the politicians in Washington, General Sherman was seeing to the Indian problems in the West. Sherman called upon Sheridan and his forces to settle the hostilities. Sheridan called upon Custer and his other experienced commanders, to do his fighting.

First, Sheridan and Custer went to Texas together. Then, they moved to Kansas. In 1868, Sheridan ordered Custer and his troops to fight the tribes of the Southern Cheyenne, Kiowas, and Arapahoes. Custer led the expedition from southern Kansas into the Oklahoma Territory. At the Washita River on November 27, 1868, Custer's men attacked a Southern Cheyenne village. He attacked at the break of dawn. Custer divided his forces to attack the village of Black Kettle from four sides. Custer led the largest wing of the attack. He succeeded in achieving total surprise, capturing the center of the camp. He then ordered the destruction of the village and its large herd of ponies.

While Custer and his men were killing the large herd of captured Indian ponies, his subordinate, Captain Frederick Benteen, worried about his friend and the regiment's second-in-command, Major Joel Elliot. Elliot was last seen going over a ridge with seventeen men riding after some escaping Indians. Major Elliot and these men were hoping to gain honors chasing the escaping Indians in that direction, or so yelled Major Elliot as he left the main body of troops.

As the ponies fell in the Indian camp, no word from Elliot was heard. Soon a much larger contingent of Indians from a larger village located a few miles away gathered on the hills above the Black Kettle village. Custer, seeing the threat, finished the disposal of the ponies. He then demonstrated a show of force with his troops by marching in the direction of these newly arrived Indians. The Indians hesitated on the hills. Custer and his men then escaped to the north before another fight ensued. With Custer trudged the surviving members of Black Kettle's tribe.

In the winter snows the troops and the Indians marched back to Fort Supply to the north. Among the captives were two Indian women: Mahwissa, the sister of Black Kettle, and Monahseetah, a young seventeen year-old Indian maiden. Mahwissa wed Custer and Monaseetah in an Indian wedding ceremony customary when one tribe defeated another. Monahseetah took the marriage seriously. Custer did not or so he wrote in his *My Life On The Plains.*

General Sheridan rode with Custer and his troops the following month.On December 11, 1868, they discovered the dead of Major Elliot's platoon. In a tight circle lying on their stomachs, feet facing feet, the small circle of troops died together, their bodies mutilated and full of arrows. Captain Benteen would forever hold Custer accountable for the loss of these men. In an open letter to the press, Benteen wrote that Custer deserted his men and left them to their fate.

Meanwhile, railroad construction continued across the territories of the Indians. The first transcontinental railroad was completed at Promontory Point, Utah, on May 10, 1869. Then the northern railroads began to survey the lands of the Dakota Territory. The Indians raided the surveying parties. To meet this challenge, General Sheridan transferred the 7th Regiment of the U. S. Cavalry to Fort Lincoln, Bismarck, Dakota Territory. The 7th was under the command of now Lieutenant- Colonel (brevet Major-General) George Custer.

In June of 1874, orders were given to explore the Black Hills. This land was known as Paha Sapa to the Indians. Custer's men discovered gold. Soon white miners were invading the sacred hills of the Indians in search of gold. By 1876, the gold rush town of Deadwood was thriving. Later that year, a former scout to Custer, while he had been stationed in Kansas, was seen in the saloons of the town. Wild

Bill Hickok was holding his famous "deadman's hand" of a queen, and two pair, aces and eights when fate dealt him a sudden end.

In the spring of 1876, much was going on around the country. Out East the nation was preparing to celebrate the Centennial in Philadelphia. Congress was holding hearings into corruption by Indian traders on Army posts in the West. Custer had been ordered back to Washington to testify before Congress.

In the meantime, President Grant had ordered Generals Sherman and Sheridan to develop a military campaign for the Dakota and Montana territories. This was to end the continuing Indian raids on the settlers and railroads. Sherman called upon General Sheridan, now head of the Military District of the Missouri headquartered in Chicago, and General George Crook in the Wyoming Territory to develop the plan. Sheridan, as usual, wanted to spearhead the campaign with Custer and his troops. Custer knew well that this was to be the last major military campaign in the Dakota Territory. He desperately wanted to lead the assault and recapture the glory that had been his at the Washita.

However, while before Congress, Custer was asked what he knew of the corruption at the posts out West. These posts were under the War Department's head, Secretary William W. Belknap. Custer openly accused Belknap and Orvil Grant, the president's brother, of profitting from the corruption at the Army posts. President Grant was furious at the accusation. President Grant ordered Generals Sherman and Sheridan to remove Custer from command of the 7th Cavalry. This included command of the expedition into the Dakota and Montana territories. Custer, fearing his career was finished, went to the White House. He sat in the lobby waiting to discuss the whole affair with President Grant, but Grant refused to see Custer.

The next day, without orders to do so, Custer caught the train back to Fort Lincoln. President Grant, upon hearing this, ordered Custer to be placed under military arrest. As he went west, Custer pleaded with his friend and superior, General Sheridan. Custer desperately needed to accompany and lead his regiment on the spring campaign.

Grant ordered Sheridan to place General Alfred Terry in command of the Dakota army. This force was to rendezvous with a Montana army, under command of Colonel John Gibbon, the same John Gibbon of Gettysburg fame. General Terry had won the battle of Fort Fisher in South Carolina in 1865, which had freed Grant's troops to encircle Petersburg in 1865 and finish the war. Grant trusted General Terry. General Terry not being an Indian fighter, asked on Custer's behalf, to have Custer lead the 7th Cavalry on this expedition. Grant relented, though he insisted that Custer remain under military arrest and subordinate to General Terry.

Custer would ride at the head of his regiment, though dark clouds in Washington remained concerning his future. As General Terry's column left Fort Lincoln on May 17, 1876, all in the command knew that Custer was in a difficult position with his superiors.

The Indians knew that the Army was planning a spring war against them. On March 17, 1876, a force of cavalry had attacked a Cheyenne camp under Chief Wooden Leg on the Powder River. In May 1876, Brigadier General George Crook left Fort Fetterman in the Wyoming Territory and headed north.

Sitting Bull and his band of Hunkpapa Sioux had joined with the Northern Cheyenne tribes and the Sioux tribes of the Minneconjou, Two Kettle, Santee, Brule, Blackfeet, and Sans Arc. The Oglala led by Crazy Horse, also joined this large gathering of Indians. During an Indian encampment, June 4 through June 7, at Deer Medicine Rocks on the Rosebud River, a large Indian sundance was held. Sitting Bull took fifty bits of flesh from each of his arms as an offering to the great *Wakan Tanka* spirit. He danced for a day and a half before nearly collapsing. He had had a great vision. He saw a large number of soldiers and horses, along with some Indians, "falling upside down into a village like grasshoppers." The

Indians celebrated as Sitting Bull's vision and his medicine were powerful guides to the tribes of the Plains.

On June 17, General Crook's column was attacked by the gathered Indians on the Rosebud. After a fierce engagement, Crook withdrew from the field heading south. He decided to regroup and reinforce. Meanwhile, the column under Terry had discovered the trail of the Indians on the Rosebud. Shortly thereafter, he rendezvoused with Colonel Gibbon's column on the Yellowstone River, to the north of the discovered trail.

Sitting Bull, and the tribes with him, decided to move from the Rosebud River valley. They proceeded to the valley of the Greasy Grass, the Little Bighorn River. Inkpaduta and his small band moved with them. Mahwissa and Monahseetah and the families of seven large camps moved with them. The vision and words of Sitting Bull moved with them. The 1862 words of Chief Little Crow, however, did not. Indeed, as Chief Little Crow had told his war council on August 17, 1862,

> ***Braves you are like little children; you know not what you are doing. You are full of the Whiteman's devil water. You are like dogs in the hot moon, when they run mad and snap at their own shadows. We are only little herds of buffaloes left scattered; the great herds that once covered the prairies are no more. See! The Whitemen are like locusts, when they fly so thick that the whole sky is as a snowstorm. You may kill one, two, ten, yes, as many as the leaves in the forest yonder, and their brothers will not miss them. Kill one, two, or ten, and ten times ten will come to kill you. Count your fingers all day long and Whitemen with guns in their hands will come faster than you can count.***

During the census of 1860, the resident population of the United States was 31,443,321. By the 1870 census, the resident population of the United States had grown to

39,818,449. On the Indian reservations and territories west of the Mississippi River, it was estimated that all Indian tribes combined numbered less than 390,000.

On June 25, 1876, there would be over 8,000 Indians in the valley of the Little Bighorn. They would confront fewer than 650 troopers and packers of the 7th Cavalry. A clash of destinies, of cultures, of warriors and troopers, and of families would see its deadly day. This would be a clash like no other. From the blood of the few would grow a cloud of locusts upon the land.

3

The Battle Plan Develops

A meeting was held on June 21, 1876, on the bank of the Yellowstone River. In attendance were General Terry, Colonel Gibbon, Lieutenant- Colonel Custer, and Major James Brisbin, Commander Second Cavalry. Per the orders issued by General Terry, a general plan for a two-pronged attack was ordered. General Terry knew a separate column under General Crook would be operating somewhere to the south. On the 21st, General Terry had not received word of General Crook's Jume 17 defeat on the Rosebud River. This action took place some one hundred miles to the south. However, General Terry knew from a scout completed by Major Reno and six companies of the 7th Cavalry the previous week that a large body of Indians was somewhere to the south. The commanders surmised the hostiles were most likely along the Rosebud Creek or the Little Bighorn River.

Custer most likely knew of Crook's column and the concept of a three-column assault on the Indians. However, given his personal predicament with President Grant, Custer probably pressured General Terry for a quick movement against the Indians. Custer needed to lead the 7th Cavalry in a crushing blow. Indeed, Custer could not afford to share glory of this campaign with Generals Terry and Crook. They were both favored in the eyes of President Grant. General Terry knew of Custer's "zeal" and "energy." He knew of Custer's desire to lead the 7th Cavalry in a dashing attack upon the Indians.

General Terry knew that a "large" Indian encampment had been discovered by the Army's Indian scouts and Reno's scout on the Rosebud River. He offered Custer, the additional four companies of the 2nd Cavalry under Major Brisbin. Custer declined. Some said Custer's trust and faith in his beloved 7th Cavalry could whip, by themselves, any Indians found on the Plains. Custer probably believed that Major Brisbin would, at best, restrict his freedom to choose battle, and hence to follow Terry's orders explicitly. At worst, Major Brisbin would be Terry's observer of Custer's actions, and therefore President Grant's observer of Custer's behavior in the field. George Armstrong Custer needed headlines with his name alone in those headlines. A certain court-martial awaited him upon completion of this campaign. Custer would need the star power of his legacy in the press to win the day when his battle in Washington took place.

On June 22, 1876, Custer and his 7th Cavalry began their portion of the battle plan. When passing Colonel Gibbon, Gibbon had shouted out to Custer to "save a few" Indians for Gibbon's column. Custer responded with a twinkle in his eye and a spur to his horse. He laughed at the suggestion as he rode away. General Terry must have had his doubts as to Custer's ability to follow his orders.

Custer headed toward the Rosebud River while Terry and Gibbon proceeded west to the Bighorn River. It was assumed that the two columns would meet somewhere on the Little Bighorn River with the hostile Indians between them. The planned date of battle was assumed to be the 26th or 27th of June.

Per Lieutenant Maguire's official report on the movements of the Terry/Gibbon column the following took place:

> ***General Terry and staff proceeded up the Yellowstone with Gibbon's column, and when near the mouth of the Big Horn the command was***

crossed to the right bank of the former stream. Gibbon's column, as now constituted, consisted of four companies of the Second Cavalry, five companies of the 7th Infantry, and Lieutenant Low's Gatling Battery, amounting in all (including the civilian employees) to 377 fighting men. The night of June 24, we passed in camp on Tulloch's Creek. The next day we crossed the divide between Tulloch's Creek, and the Big Horn, and reached the latter stream after a severe march of twenty-two miles. The country was exceedingly rough, hill after hill and ravine after ravine, but with little grass and plenty of the ubiquitous sage and cactus. The soil was alkaline, and the air was filled with dust, clogging up the nostrils, ears, and throat. In addition to this, the day was very warm, and not a drop of water to be obtained on the march. The infantry had understood that we were to follow Tulloch's Creek, and knowing that in that case they could obtain water at any time they did not fill their canteens. The consequence was that they suffered terribly, and numbers of men toward the close of the march dropped on the way, utterly exhausted. The refreshing sight of the Big Horn finally gladdened their hearts, and those on the road having been brought in, they remained in camp that night. General Terry, taking the cavalry, pushed on, and a most wearisome and disheartening march we made of it. The night was black, and a cold rain drenched us. Besides this, we were obliged to cross a very rough country; and the descent and ascent of steep declivities, with no other guide than the occasional white horse, (if so lucky as to get directly behind one,) was anything but pleasant. The Indian scouts finally found a pool of alkaline water after a march of 12 miles, and we encamped in the mud for the short remaining portion of the night. About 11 o'clock the following

> ***morning (June 26) we were joined by the infantry near the mouth of the Little Big Horn, and we then proceeded up the valley of that river. We went into camp that night only after the infantry had made a march of more than 50 miles in two days. The next morning the march was resumed, and we sighted two teepees in the valley . . . .***

As Lieutenant Maguire put in his report, the journey from the mouth of the Rosebud River on the Yellowstone River to the mouth of the Bighorn proceeded without incident from Indian forces. The biggest threats and enemies to this column were the torturous country and dry conditions affecting the men. The march was hard for infantry on foot. The miles averaged per day varied depending of the roughness of the country adjacent to the rivers. The miles covered during a ten-to twelve-hour day were realized at the expense of great exhaustion. On better terrain the column might make thirty miles. Lieutenant Maguire recorded the column's movements. Gibbon's infantry covered fifty miles in two grueling days.

General Terry, knowing Custer's 7th Cavalry would be moving quickly, needed to push ahead with Major Brisbin's 2nd Cavalry contingent. The infantry, though well armed with the three Gatling guns and the men's Springfield "Long Tom" single-shot, breech-loading muskets, were painfully slow in their movements. Terry knew, as did Custer, that the infantry and Gatling guns moved slowly. Major Reno had taken the Gatling guns along with his six companies of cavalry the previous week., That march was slowed greatly by the Gatling guns. Indeed, Major Reno could have covered nearly twice the territory he did without the Gatling guns. When deep ravines and gullies were traversed, the Gatling guns would have to be carefully manhandled down and up these terrain features. For the quick-tempoed cavalry, these delays were unforgiveable.

Infantry of the day could be assumed to move at roughly three miles per hour over good terrain. Cavalry at a company trot could move about eight miles an hour. At a lope, between a trot and a gallop, cavalry could move about ten to twelve miles per hour. At a gallop, usually reserved for charges, or hasty retreats, cavalry could move between fifteen and thirty miles per hour, though for short distances.

Per the *1862 U. S. Army Manual* for the cavalry called *Cavalry Tactics*, written by Brigadier- General Philip St. George Cooke, cavalry tactics and training were to be consistent throughout the Army. General Cooke had observed European cavalry tactics prior to the Civil War and wrote this manual per the War Department's instruction. He served as a cavalry division commander in the Civil War. His son served with the Confederate Army. His daughter was married to General Jeb Stuart, head of Lee's Confederate Cavalry.

Per the Army manual, the horses on long marches needed to be rested every hour for a short duration of ten to fifteen minutes. Even with these short rest periods, the cavalry could move over longer distances than the infantry. General Terry must have had growing concerns as to his column's slow progress up the Bighorn River. The rapid movement of Custer's column might bring him to battle before Terry could catch up. Terry probably knew Custer would find the Indian encampment on the 26th, if not the 25th. It was looking like Terry and Gibbon would not find the Little Bighorn Indian camp until the 27th.

Still the columns moved on. On the morning of the 25th, Terry and Gibbon were at least thirty-five to forty miles north of the Indian village. By late afternoon on the 25th, the column must have been at least twenty-five to thirty miles north of the village.

Meanwhile, Custer and his column proceeded up the Rosebud River valley. Per Lieutenant Wallace's report the following occurred:

At 12 p.m. on the 22nd of June, 1876, the 7th Cavalry, under Lieutenant-Colonel Custer, left camp on the Yellowstone and moved up that stream for 2 miles to the mouth of the Rosebud, then up the Rosebud. We crossed the latter near its mouth. It was a clear running stream, from 3 to 4 feet wide, and about 3 inches deep; bottom gravel, but in many places water standing in pools. Water slightly alkaline. Owing to delays with the pack-train the command moved only about 12 miles that day. We camped on the left bank of the Rosebud, at the base of a steep bluff. We had plenty of wood and water, and grass for our animals. During the greater part of the march the trail followed the high ground, or second bottom, where the soil was poor, the grass thin, and crowded out by sage-brush and cactus. In the lower part of the valley the soil appeared to be good, the grazing fair, the bottom timbered with large cottonwood. Small willows grew thickly along the banks in many places. For the first 8 miles the hills sloped back gradually, but near camp were more abrupt, and covered with stones and cactus. Several deep ravines were crossed during the day. The only serious obstacle to a wagon-train would be the numerous crossings of the bends of the Rosebud. Weather clear, but not unpleasantly warm. No game visible. Plenty of fish in the creek.

June 23, 1876. – Orders were given last night that trumpet signals would be discontinued, that the stable-guards would wake their respective companies at 3 a.m., and the command would move at 5 a.m. General Custer stated that short marches would be made for the first few days, after that they would be increased. All were ready at the appointed time, and the command moving out we crossed to

the right bank of the Rosebud. The bluff being very broken, we had to follow the valley for some distance, crossing the Rosebud five times in 3 miles; thence up the right side for about 10 miles. There we halted, to allow the pack-train to close up. Soon after starting, crossed to the left bank and followed that for 15 miles, and camped on the right bank at 4:30 p.m., making a distance of over 30 miles. The last of the pack-train did not get into camp until near sunset. About 5 miles from our last camp we came to the trail made by Major Reno, a few days previous, and a few miles further on saw the first traces of the Indian camps. They were all old, but everything indicated a large body of Indians. Every bend of the stream bore traces of some old camp, and their ponies had nipped almost every spear of grass. The ground was strewn with broken bones and cuttings from buffalo hides. The country passed over after the first few miles was rolling, and poor, except along the creek. Grass all eaten up. Plenty of cottonwood along the creek. During the last 5 or 6 miles of the march, the cottonwood timber was gradually replaced by ash and a species of elder. The valley was about one-fourth of a mile wide, and for the last 15 miles the hills were very steep and rocky, sandstone being present. The country back from the hills looked to be very much broken. The hills were covered with a short growth of pines. No game seen during the day; weather warm and clear.

June 24, 1876.- The command moved at 5 a.m. this morning. After we had been on the march about an hour, our Crow scouts came in and reported fresh signs of Indians, but in no great numbers. After a short consultation, General Custer, with an escort of two companies, moved out in advance,

the remainder of the command following at a distance of about half a mile. We followed the right bank of the Rosebud; crossed two running tributaries, the first we had seen. At 1 p.m. the command was halted, scouts sent ahead, and the men made coffee. The scouts got back about 4, and reported a fresh camp at the forks of the Rosebud. Everything indicated that the Indians were not more than thirty miles away. At 5 p.m. the command moved out; crossed to the left bank of Rosebud; passed through several large camps. The trail now was fresh, and the whole valley scratched up by the trailing lodge-poles. At 7:45 p.m. we encamped on the right bank of Rosebud. Scouts were sent ahead to see which branch of the stream the Indians had followed. Distance marched to-day, about 28 miles. Soil in the valley very good, and in many places grazing very fine. Timber scattering, principally elder and ash. Hills rough and broken, and thickly covered with pines. Weather clear and very warm. About 9 p.m. the scouts returned and reported that the Indians had crossed the divide to the Little Big Horn River. General Custer determined to cross the divide that night (the 24th), to conceal the command, the next day (the 25th) find out the locality of the village, and attack the following morning (the 26th) at daylight. Orders were given to move at midnight, but we did not get off until near 1 a.m., and, owing to delays on account of pack-train, we had only marched about 8 miles when daylight appeared. We halted, and the men were ordered to make coffee. While waiting here a scout came back from Lieutenant Varnum, who had been sent out the night before. In a note to General Custer, Lieutenant Varnum stated that he could see the smoke of the village about 20 miles away, on the

Little Big Horn. The scout pointed out the butte from which the village could be seen. It was about 8 miles ahead.

We moved on, and when near the butte Lieutenant Varnum joined us and reported that the Indians had discovered the command and that he had seen couriers go in the direction of the village. General Custer assembled the officers, told them what he had heard, and said he would move ahead and attack the village without further delay.

At 12 p.m., on the 25th, we crossed the divide between the Rosebud and Little Big Horn. From the divide could be seen the valley of the Little Big Horn, and about 15 or 20 miles to the north-west could be seen a light blue cloud, and to the practiced eyes showed that our game was near. A small stream starting from the point near where we crossed the divide flowed in the direction of the smoke. After assignment of battalions was made, General Custer followed down the right bank of the stream, and Major Reno the left. When within three miles of the Little Big Horn, Major Reno was ordered across to the right bank and the two columns moved together for some distance, when Major Reno was ordered ahead. He recrossed this stream, moved down it, crossed the Little Big Horn, halted his command, formed line and moved down the valley and commenced the battle of June 25.

In passing from the Rosebud to the Little Big Horn, we followed up the left branch of the first, then up a dry ravine to the crest of the divide; grass short, soil poor, hills low. From the crest to the Little Big Horn the country was broken and the valley

narrow; some timber along the little stream we followed down. Distance traveled during the night of the 24th and on the 25th about 6 miles.

Some observations come from reading the above report by Lieutenant Wallace. He, along with Lieutenant Maguire, were the regiment's engineers. By this assignment, both Lieutenant Wallace and Lieutenant Maguire were responsible for maintaining an accurate log of the movements of the two columns. Lieutenant Wallace was accurate in the time recordings of the Custer column. At the Reno Court of Inquiry two and a half years later, testimonies would vary as to times of day. Some in the column kept their watches to Chicago time. Lieutenant Wallace maintained his watch to local Montana time. When comparing his times to present-day daylight savings times of sunrise and sunset for Billings, Montana, his times are the most consistent of those who kept time on their watches. Sunrise is at 5:24 a.m. on June 24th, while sunset is at 9:07 p.m.. Those familiar with the northern lattitudes in June know first light occurs about 40 minutes before official sunrise. Twilight visibility exists for about 40 minutes after official sunset.

Custer wanted to take advantage of the long days of June. He would awaken his column about 3:00 a.m. and be on the march by 5:00 a.m. His cavalry could cover thirty miles by 4:30 p.m. However, he was encumbered by the movement of his pack-train. Per civilian packer B. I. Churchill's testimony at the Reno Court of Inquiry, the pack-train consisted of 175 mules and six or seven civilian packers. This pack-train could be strung out for over two miles depending on terrain and the movement of the column. Custer would quite often be impatient with this encumbrance. He would move ahead with either a scouting contingent of troopers or with the advanced Indian scouts under Lieutenant Varnum's command. When Custer and his cavalry reached temporary camp on the 24th at 4:30 p.m., it took until nearly dark, around 9:40 p.m., for the pack-train to catch up with Custer per Lieutenant Wallace's observation.

When the Indian scouts came to Custer on the night of the 24th, Custer was provided with intelligence that the hostile Indians were about thirty miles away. In other words, the village was within a hard day's ride on the 25th. This made the possibility of an early morning attack by Custer's men on the 26th likely. Custer knowing of the distance and difficulties experienced by his column in the valley of the Rosebud, probably figured that General Terry and Colonel Gibbon's column could not be in the village area until the 27th at the earliest. The infantry and Gatling guns were slow movers. In addition, the scouts had no sign of advanced elements of Crook's column coming up from the Wyoming Territory. In fact, Crook's column had engaged the Indians along the Rosebud farther upstream (south), on June 17th. Thus an attack on the Indian camp on the 26th, would be Custer's alone. Custer would go first.

Meanwhile in the immense Indian village, the Indians were celebrating the victory of June 17th. This battle was known to the Cheyenne as "Where the Young Girl Saved Her Brother". Cheyenne Chief, Comes In Sight, had been rescued from certain death at the hands of Crook's men and their Crow scouts by his sister, Buffalo Calf Road Woman. She had ridden into the heat of battle to rescue a stranded Comes In Sight. Indeed such Indian bravery was to be celebrated. Many from the huge gathered village danced into the late evening of the 24th.

Sitting Bull knew that the battle of the 17th, did not represent the vision he had seen at Deer Medicine Rocks. He decided to go off by himself. High on a hill across the river, a hill later to be known by the name of one of Custer's officers, Sitting Bull fashioned some medicine bags of deer skin, with tobacco and willow bark inside. He attached these to willow sticks. Along with a few stones he found and stacked on the hill, he stuck the medicine bags into the high ground of Weir Point.

In the village, Mahwissa, Monahseetah, and her child, Yellow Bird, were tending to their tribal duties in the camp of the Southern Cheyennes. Buffalo Calf Road Woman and her husband, Black Coyote, were likewise in camp that night. The hours ahead on this new day were about to forever change their lives.

4

What Was He Thinking?

As one reads Lieutenant Wallace's description of events on the 24th, the coincidence of Custer's own words from his *My Life On The Plains* becomes fascinating for the modern-day reader. Written in 1873, five years after the Washita, and three years before the Little Bighorn, George Armstrong Custer had a most theatrical way of telling his story of the march and the battle. I will let his own words speak, only editing specific references to locations encountered on the way to the Washita, and to individuals who were with Custer during that 1868 campaign. The words are hauntingly foredooming of the actions that led to the Battle of the Little Bighorn. It was as if he was writing Lieutenant Wallace's report for him -only years before.

Read and listen as George Armstrong Custer describes his actions before the battle.

> ***(I)n the distance I descried a horseman approaching us as rapidly as his tired steed could carry him. . . . What tidings would he bring? Was my first thought . . . Perhaps he has discovered an Indian trail -a fresh one . . . . If a trail has been discovered, then woe unto the luckless Indians . . .for so long as that remains and the endurance of men and horses holds out, just so long we will follow that***

trail, until the pursuer and pursued are brought face to face or the one or the other succumbs to the fatigues and exhaustion of the race.

These and a host of kindred thoughts flashed in rapid succession through my mind as soon as I had discovered the distant approach of the scout, for the scout I knew it must be. As yet none of the command had observed his coming, not being on as high ground as where I stood. By means of my field glass I was able to make out the familiar form of . . . one of the scouts. After due waiting, when minutes seemed like hours, the scout galloped up to where I was waiting and in a few hurried, almost breathless words informed me that the trail of an Indian war party . . . was not twenty-four hours old. . . . Here was news of a desirable character....

. . . My resolution was formed in a moment and as quickly put in train of execution. (I) summoned all the officers to report at once. There was no tardiness on their part for while they had not heard the report brought in by the scout they had witnessed his unexpected arrival and his equally sudden departure– circumstances which told them plainer than mere words that something unusual was in the air. The moment they were all assembled about me I acquainted them the intelligence received . . . and at the same time informed them that we would at once set out to join in the pursuit, a pursuit which could and would only end when we overtook our enemies. And in order that we should not be trammelled in our movements it was my intention then and there to abandon our train . . . taking with us only such supplies as we could carry on our persons and strapped to our saddles. The train would be left under the

protection of about eighty men detailed from the different troops and under the command of one officer, to whom orders would be given to follow us with the train as rapidly as the character of our route would permit. Each trooper was to carry with him one hundred rounds of ammunition . . . We were to move in light marching order as far as this was practicable.

Then taking out my watch, the officers were notified that in twenty minutes from that time, "The advance" would be (given) and the march in pursuit begun– the intervening time to be devoted to carrying out the instructions just given. In a moment every man and officer in the command was vigorously at work preparing to set out for a rough ride, the extent or result of which no one could foresee. . . . The most inferior of the horses were selected to fill up the detail of . . . cavalry which was to remain and escort the train. . . . All felt that a great opportunity was before us, and to improve it only required determination and firmness on our part. How thoroughly and manfully every demand of this kind was responded to by my command. . . .

. . .Before proceeding to narrate the incidents of the pursuit which led us to the battle . . . I will refer to the completion of our hasty preparations to detach ourselves from the encumbrance of our immense . . . train. In the last chapter (Chapter Nine of My Life On The Plains*) it has been seen that the train was to be left behind under the protection of an officer and eighty cavalrymen, with orders to push after us, following our trail . . . as rapidly as the teams could move. Where or when it would join us no one could foretell; in*

all probability, however, not until the pursuit had terminated and we had met and vanquished our savage foes or had been defeated by them.

. . . Under existing orders the guard for the protection of our train was each day under the command of the officer of the day, the tour of duty of the latter continuing twenty-four hours, beginning in the morning. . . .

. . . Everything being in readiness to set out, at the expiration of the alloted twenty minutes "The advance" was (given) and the pursuit on our part began. . . .

. . . After leaving the . . . train we continued our march rapidly. . . . No halt was made during the day either for rest or refreshment. . . . Could it be that the Indians had discovered that they were pursued, and had broken up into smaller parties or changed the direction of their trail?

. . . We had hurried along, our interest increasing with each mile passed over. . . .

. . . Our scouts and Indian guides were kept far out in front . . . to discover, if possible the trail. At last one of the scouts gave the signal that the trail had been discovered and in a few moments the command had reached it and we were now moving with lighter and less anxious heart. . . . A free rein was given to our horses as we hastened along. . . .

. . . I could see we were gradually descending into a valley, probably of some stream, and far in advance appeared the dim outline of timber, such as usually fringes the banks of many western

streams. Selecting a few well mounted troopers and some of the scouts, I directed them to set out at a moderate gallop. . . .

. . . Satisfied now that we were on the right course, our anxiety lessened, but our interest increased.

. . . We began our preparations in the most quiet manner to resume the pursuit. No bugle calls were permitted as in this peculiar country sound travels a long distance and we knew not but that our wily foes were located near by. Before starting I conferred with our Indian allies, all of whom were firmly convinced that our enemy's village was probably not far away, and most likely was in the valley in which we then were, as the trail for some miles had led us down the stream on whose banks we halted . . . . To my surprise the Indian scouts advised that we delay further pursuit. . . . When asked for the reasons for favoring such a course they could give none of a satisfactory nature. I then concluded that this disinclination to continue the pursuit . . . arose from the natural reluctance, shared by all Indians, to attack an unseen foe, whether concealed in darkness or other natural or artificial means of shelter. . . .

. . . As soon as each troop was in readiness to resume the pursuit the troop commander reported the fact to headquarters. . . . Silently the command stretched out its long length as the troopers filed off . . . . To prevent the possibility of the command coming precipitately upon our enemies the . . . scouts were directed to keep three or four hundred yards in advance of all others . . . then came . . . the white scouts. . . . With these I rode, that I might be as near the advance guard as possible.

The cavalry followed in rear at the distance of a quarter or half a mile. . . .

. . . Orders were given prohibiting even a word being uttered above a whisper. . . . In this silent manner we rode mile after mile. Occasionally an officer would ride by my side and whisper some inquiry or suggestion, but aside from this our march was unbroken by sound or deed. At last we discovered that our . . . guides in front had halted and were awaiting my arrival. Word was quietly sent to halt the column until inquiry in front could be made. . . .

. . .Where were they at that moment? Perhaps sleeping. . . . It was almost certain to our minds that the Indians we had been pursuing were the builders of the fire. Were they still there and asleep? We were too near already to attempt to withdraw undiscovered. Our only course was to determine the facts at once, and be prepared for the worst. . . .

. . . If Indians, as then seemed highly probable, were sleeping . . . our scouts would arouse them. . . . The matter was soon determined. Our scouts soon arrived . . . and discovered it (the Indian camp site) to be deserted. . . . Again we set out, this time more cautiously, if possible, than before, the command and scouts moving at a greater distance in rear.

. . . In order to judge of the situation more correctly I this time accompanied the scouts. Silently we advanced, I mounted, they upon foot, keeping at the head of my horse. . . .

"What is it?" I inquired as soon as (the scout) reached my horse's side. "Heap Injuns down there," pointing in the direction from which he had just come.

. . . Looking in the direction indicated, I could distinctly recognize the presence of a large body of animals of some kind in the valley below. . . .

. . . I looked at them long and anxiously, the guide uttering not a word, but was unable to discover anything in their appearance different from what might be presented by a herd of buffaloes under similar circumstances . . . I inquired in a low tone why he thought there were Indians there. "Me heard dog bark," was the satisfactory reply. Indians are noted for the large number of dogs always found in their villages, but never accompanying their war parties. . . .

. . . I waited quietly to be convinced; I was assured, but wanted to be doubly so. I was rewarded in a moment by hearing the barking of a dog in the heavy timber off to the right. . . . I turned to retrace my steps when another sound was borne to my ear . . . it was the distant cry of an infant; and savages though they were and justly outlawed by the number and atrocity of their present murders and depredations on the helpless settlers of the frontier, I could not but regret that in a war such as we were forced to engage in the mode and circumstances of battle would possibly prevent discrimination.

. . . I hastened back . . . and a message sent back to halt the cavalry, enjoining complete silence and directing every officer to ride to the point we

then occupied. . . . Soon they came and after dismounting and collecting in a little circle I informed them of what I had seen and heard; and in order that they might individually learn as much as possible of the character of the ground and the location of the village I proposed that all should . . . proceed gently to the crest and there obtain a view of the valley beyond. This was done; not a word was spoken until we crouched together. . . . In whispers I briefly pointed out everything that was to be seen, . . . then . . . the plan of the attack was explained to all and each assigned his part.

. . . The general plan was to employ the hours between then and daylight to completely surround the village and at daybreak, or as soon as it was barely light enough for the purpose, to attack the Indians from all sides. The command . . . was divided into four nearly equal detachments. Two of them set out at once, as they had each to make a circuitous march of several miles in order to arrive at the points assigned them from which to make their attack. The third detachment moved to its position . . . and until that time remained with the main or fourth column. This last, whose movements I accompanied, was to make the attack from the point from which we had first discovered the . . . village.

. . . By this disposition it was hoped to prevent the escape of every inmate of the village. . . .

. . . With the suspicion so natural and peculiar to the Indian nature, they (the Indian scouts) had, in discussing the proposed attack upon the Indian village, concluded that we would be outnumbered by the occupants of the village, who of

course would fight with the utmost desperation in defense of their lives and lodges, and to prevent a complete defeat of our forces or to secure a drawn battle we might be induced to engage in a parley with the hostile tribe(s). . .

. . . They (the Indian scouts) also mistrusted the ability of the whites to make a successful attack upon a hostile village, located, as this one was known to be, in heavy timber, and aided by the natural banks of the stream. Disaster seemed certain in the minds of the (Indian scouts) to follow us, if we attacked a force of unknown strength and numbers. . .

. . . Before advancing . . . strict orders were issued prohibiting the firing of a single shot until the signal to attack should be made. . . . The other three detachments had been informed before setting out that the main column would attack . . . without waiting to ascertain whether they were in position or not. In fact it would be impracticable to communicate with either of the first two until the attack began. . . .

. . . In this order we began to descend the slope leading down to the village. The distance to the timber in the valley below proved greater than it had appeared to the eye. . . . We had approached near enough to the village now to plainly catch a view here and there of the tall white lodges as they stood in irregular order. . . . From the openings at the top of some of them we could perceive faint columns of smoke ascending, the occupants no doubt having kept their feeble fires during the entire night. We had approached so near the village that from the dead silence which reigned I

feared the lodges were deserted, the Indians having fled before we advanced. I was about to turn in my saddle and direct the signal for the attack to be given, still anxious as to where the other detachments were, when a single rifle shot rang sharp and clear on the far side of the village from where we were.

. . . In this manner the battle . . . commenced. The bugles sounded the charge and the entire command dashed rapidly into the village. The Indians were caught napping. . . .

Had Custer managed to get into the Indian village on the Little Bighorn River, the following would most likely have been his thoughts:

. . . Realizing at once the dangers of their situation, they quickly overcame their first surprise and in an instant seized their rifles, bows, and arrows, and . . . while some leaped . . . using the bank as a rifle-pit began a vigorous and determined defense. . . . Actual possession of the village and its lodges was ours within a few moments after the charge was made, but this was an empty victory unless we could vanquish the late occupants, who were then pouring in a rapid and well directed fire from their stations behind trees and banks. At the first onset a considerable number of the Indians rushed from the village in the direction from which (one of the columns) had attacked. . . .

. . . We had gained the center of the village and were in the midst of the lodges, while on all sides could be heard the sharp crack of the Indian rifles and the heavy responses from the carbines of the troopers. . . .

These were the words George Armstrong Custer used to describe his battle on the Washita River. These are the reflected events on November 26 and 27, 1868. They were put to pen and paper five years later in 1873 and 1874. Key words reappeared many times in the testimonies of men who rode with Custer on that fateful day of June 25, 1876, at the Reno Court of Inquiry. There was reference to a "sleeping village," "dogs barking," a "deserted" look to the village just prior to the attack. These all would be recalled in the testimonies of those who rode with Custer and were called on to testify in 1879.

Trumpeter John Martin was Custer's trumpeter on June 25. He was one of the last four troopers of Custer's battalion to see and hear Custer before his attack from the Medicine Tail Coulee. Martin survived the Battle of the Little Bighorn. He recalled at Reno's Court of Inquiry these words:

"Custer now made a speech to his men saying, 'We will go down and make a crossing (of the Little Bighorn River) and capture the village.' The whole command pulled off their hats and cheered. . . ."

These words were given to the two columns of men that Custer had with him. He stated them after the command had halted on the high bluffs overlooking the village on the Little Bighorn. These were the very same thoughts Custer had when at the Washita. These thoughts were most likely his when he went into battle at the Little Bighorn.

5

The Southern Battles of the Little Bighorn

On June 24, while Sitting Bull was sitting on the high hill now known as Weir Point setting his medicine rocks and pouches, Custer's Indian wife, Monahseetah, and Custer's child by Monahseetah, Yellow Bird, were in the large Indian village on the Little Bighorn. Here they watched as the large circles of Indian camps celebrated victory over Gray Fox Crook and his column the week before.

Twenty miles away to the east, on a small creek now known as Middle Fork of Davis Creek, an eight year-old Indian boy named Deeds, along with his companions, Brown Back and Drags the Rope, were tending to their ponies. The nearby grasses and water found along this area between the Little Bighorn and the Rosebud were some of the last left after the large village had passed by here a few days before.

A short distance to the north and east of these Indian boys, Custer's column had stopped at 7:45 p.m. They were on the west bank of the Rosebud, a short distance from the mouth of Davis Creek, near current-day Busby. Custer's Crow Indian scouts knew that the large village of hostile Indians would have crossed from the Rosebud to the Little Bighorn via the trail known as Lodgepole Trail. As one looks at current maps of the land farther south along the Rosebud, the topography of the Wolf Mountains a few miles south of

Davis Creek would prevent easy crossings. Sioux tribes, as did the Crows, well knew of this trail.

Scouts Mitch Bouyer, Fred Girard, Charley Reynolds, George Herenden, Isaiah Dorman, and the Crow and Arikara (known as Rees) Indian scouts, were under the command of Lieutenant Charles A. Varnum. As Custer conferred with them that evening, he decided to send the scouts ahead to verify the Indian trail and its direction. By 9:00 p.m. word came back to Custer that the village had passed this way to the valley of the Little Bighorn.

Custer decided that heading farther south would be futile per Terry's original orders. Terry had ordered Custer to go to the head of the Tongue River. Custer knew from the scouts' reports that his column was at most a day's march from the village. He would press ahead that night, the 24th, and during the day of June 25 scout the village for avenues of attack. Custer's plan was for an early morning assault on the 26th. This plan was relayed to the officers of the 7th Cavalry per Lieutenant Wallace's report on the movement of Custer's column along the Rosebud.

Custer wanted the column to be ready to move at 11:00 p.m. But as Lieutenant Wallace recorded, due to delays with the pack-train. the column did not get off until 1:00 a.m. on the 25th. It was dark and the movement difficult. Though the Indian guides had said this was the easiest crossing point to get to the Little Bighorn, the column, especially the pack-train of mules, found the going slow. Company F, under the command of Captain George Yates was in charge of the pack-train this day.

At some point, probably close to the junction of the Middle Fork and the main Davis Creek, a box or two, one filled with Army hardtack, fell from one of the mules. It was dark and the mules difficult to control, therefore, the boxes on the ground were not noticed by the column of troopers.

As progress of the column was painfully slow, Custer decided to ride ahead with the scouts to the high ground known as the Crow's Nest. Lieutenant Varnum had climbed it with his scouts hours before. It was from here that first views of the valley of the Little Bighorn River could be made.

As first daylight appeared around 4:45 a.m., the Indian scouts pointed out to Lieutenant Varnum, and later to Custer, the early morning blue smoke of the village campfires. The village was approximately fifteen miles to the northwest. Beyond the smoke was a large, dark, moving mass. The Indian scouts could see the twenty thousand ponies of an immense herd. Custer, even with his field glasses, could only make out a dark mass of something -maybe a large buffalo herd.

About this time, Quartermaster Sergeant Curtis from Company F noticed the missing packs from the mules. He reported this to his commanding officer, Captain Yates. The missing packs were somewhere behind, along the columns's trail. Captain Yates reported this to his friend, and senior officer, Captain Myles Keogh. Keogh, knowing that Custer did not want any disclosure of his column to the hostile Indians, sought out Custer and found his adjutant, Lieutenant W. W. Cooke. Sergeant Curtis was ordered to take a couple of troopers and go back along the trail and retrieve the missing packs.

As Sergeant Curtis and his detail rounded a bend near the Rosebud and Davis Creek intersection, they found an Indian sitting over an opened box of hardtack. They drew their weapons and fired. They killed the Indian over the box. These were the first shots of the Battle of the Little Bighorn. As the troopers recovered the packs, they noticed two more Indians over a hill, and again fired their weapons. These Indians they missed.

Quickly the two young Indians ran on foot to the northwest. With anger and fear in their hearts, they headed through the ravines and open ground leading back to the large village. The troopers were aware that Indians now knew of the column's presence and rode quickly back to find Captain Yates.

Meanwhile, as they ran, Brown Back and Drags The Rope, mourned for their dead, young friend. Deeds. Deeds was the first to die that soon-to-be-hot June 25th. He would not be the last.

Sergeant Curtis found Captain Yates and reported the incident. All officers knew that Custer would need to know of this quickly. Custer in his high perch on Crow's Nest was some two miles up the trail. Someone, though no one remembered who, ordered the column to advance and find Custer. Captain Tom Custer was at the head of this column when it approached the Crow's Nest.

Scout Fred Girard descended the high ground with General Custer. At the Reno Court of Inquiry he recalled seeing Tom Custer in front of the moving column. General Custer asked Girard and himself aloud, "Who in the mischief moved that command?" When brother George met brother Tom, who was then sixty yards in front of the column, Girard heard General Custer ask, "Tom, who moved the command?" Captain Custer replied, "I don't know, the orders were to march and we marched."

As this discussion was taking place, Lieutenant Varnum and scout Charley Reynolds saw a dozen or so warriors on a rise to the north and west. Charley Reynolds pointed to the retreating Indians and yelled out to Custer, "There go your Indians skedaddling!"

Custer now knew that his column had been detected. His greatest fear was being realized. Before he could have his great victory, the Indian village would soon be on the "jump" in all directions.

Custer called for a quick officer's call at the base of the Crow's Nest while the command was still in the Davis Creek valley. The column was still hidden from Indian observation. He evaluated the latest events, both these last seen Indians, as well as the few observed along the column's trail behind them. There would be no time to do a full day's scout of the village ahead. Rather, the column would be divided into four battalions. Guard of the pack-train would be shifted to Captain Thomas McDougall's Company B. For added protection of the pack-train, one NCO and six troopers from each company, a total of eighty-four, would be assigned to help guard the slow moving pack-train. Custer ordered that all of the men carry with them 100 rounds of carbine cartridges, as well as twenty-four revolver rounds. Custer would have his battalions advance while leaving the slow pack-train to follow in the trail of his column. These orders were recalled by many at the RCOI.

The four battalions would be assigned as follows: Major Reno would command Companies A, M, and G. Captain Benteen would be assigned his own Company H as well as Companies D, and K. Custer would have another detachment headed by Captain Myles Keogh with his Company I and Companies L and C. Captain Yates would head up the last detachment with his Company F and Company E. His would be short a company, as Company B, usually assigned to the Yates battalion was with the pack-train. Custer would personally lead the last two battalions, those of Keogh and Yates.

The column mounted up at the base of the Crow's Nest. The time was about noon per Lieutenant Wallace's watch. Within a mile the column crossed the divide between the Rosebud and the Little Bighorn valleys. The men in the column had their first view of the valley that would forever change their lives.

Shortly after crossing the high ground of the divide, the column began descending through a valley that was the headwaters of a small creek. Once known as Ash Creek, for the ash trees found along its banks, this creek would become known as Reno Creek. Like most creek valleys of the western plains, the way was meandering and lined with brush and increasing numbers of timber. Custer's words of his descent into the valley of the Washita years before must have been crossing his mind.

The column moved forward about eight miles per the recollections of Captain Benteen, and Lieutenant Edward Godfrey, commander of Company K. Just after a point where Reno Creek changes direction from running northwest to a southwesterly course, Custer halted the column. It was in a deep valley surrounded by high hills as Captain Benteen recalled at the Reno Court of Inquiry. Here Custer detached Captain Benteen's battalion. Custer needed to check the high ground to his left. Lingering in his mind were the orders of General Terry to constantly feel to his left to ensure no Indians escaped to the south. Perhaps Custer wanted to make sure General Crook and his column were not in the area.

Captain Benteen was not made aware of Terry's orders or of Custer's necessity to gain victory. He would forever accuse Custer of needlessly sending him on a useless hunt of valleys. As Benteen stated at the Reno Court of Inquiry "valley hunting, ad infinitum." But, Benteen followed his orders.

About a half mile after Benteen departed, Custer had a better view of the country in front of Benteen. Custer sent an updated order to Captain Benteen. This message served directly to have Benteen continue moving on his southwesterly direction. Indirectly, when the messenger returned to Custer, Custer had an approximate time measure of how far Benteen could travel over a mile distance in this country. The messenger sent was Custer's regimental Chief Trumpeter Henry Voss.

As Benteen proceeded another mile along his southwesterly trek, a second message was received from Custer. This was via the regiment's sergeant major, W. W. Sharrow. This message again emphasized Custer's order to keep searching the valleys in front of Benteen. As Sergeant Major Sharrow returned, Custer now had a second time measure in his head to gage Benteen's progress and whereabouts. This would be crucial knowledge for Custer if Benteen was needed later in the fight.

One may ask why Custer sent Benteen off in such a direction? Besides the Terry order to constantly feel to the left, from the scouts' reports the Indian village most likely was directly in front of his advancing column per Custer's way of thinking. With Benteen to the south, Benteen could then "pitch into any Indians" he found there. Custer could then determine where best to strike the village in a multi-pronged attack with the other battalions. As Benteen proceeded with his detachment, his last view of Custer's column was the last company of Company E. Company E rode the gray horses. Benteen distinctly remembered this at the RCOI.

As Custer proceeded down Reno Creek, he advanced Major Reno's battalion to the left side of the creek to ride parallel to Custer's column on the right side of the creek. Many troopers later recalled this portion of the advance. The columns soon came to a morass which made for a watering hole for the horses. Custer warned his men to take a short break of no more than five minutes, as the horses would need to gallop shortly. Too much water would encumber the beasts.

About a mile further down the creek a lone teepee was spotted. Inside was the decorated, dead body of Chief Old She Bear. Old She Bear had been wounded at the Rosebud battle with Gray Fox Crook the previous week and had passed away during the night.

Unknown to Custer or his scouts, a small band of seven lodges of Cheyenne Indians was close by. With forty or so Indians, Chief Little Wolf, had just visited this same teepee. Little Wolf had seen the dust of the approaching soldiers. He hurriedly set off to warn the large village just over three and a half miles away.

As Custer and his men came over the ridge unaware of Little Wolf's band, they explored the teepee and its contents. Suddenly, off to the right on another rise, another group of Indians was seen by the scouts. They set off on a "jump" as Trumpeter Martin recalled. Fred Girard yelled out to Custer, "Here are your Indians, running like devils!"

The wheel of battle was beginning to turn more rapidly now. Custer summoned Major Reno to cross the creek and hear Custer's latest order. Without the precise intelligence Custer needed as to the location and size of the village, Custer could only guess as to its exact whereabouts. Having sent Captain Benteen to the south with orders to "pitch into any Indians" he found there, Custer must have assumed that the middle of the village would be directly in front of him. As they headed west along Reno Creek. Custer ordered Major Reno to move forward rapidly along the creek and "pitch into" any Indians he found.

As Reno returned to his detachment, he ordered them forward at a fast trot. Custer halted his column. He summoned Lieutenant Varnum and the Indian scouts. Custer ordered them to advance with Reno. They were to attack and capture the large pony herd on the high steppe beyond the village. The Indian scouts were free to take as war prizes as many ponies as they could handle. Custer then summoned his adjutant, Lieutenant Cooke, and his now second-in-command of the Custer column, Captain Keogh. Custer gave them instructions to ride ahead with Reno to the Little Bighorn River and observe Reno's crossing at the ford. The ford was then about two and a half miles in their front. Lieutenant Cooke was told to inform Major Reno that when Reno attacked, Custer would support him with Custer's "entire column."

Custer at sometime between ordering Reno to advance and leaving the lone teepee instructed Captain George Yates and his battalion to burn and destroy the lone teepee. After ensuring its destruction Yates was to catch up to Custer and report its destruction.

As Lieutenant Cooke and Captain Keogh rode off in pursuit of Reno's column, Sergeant Daniel Kanipe, riding with the now trailing company of Company C, pointed out to First Sergeant Edwin Bobo Indians on the bluffs to the column's right. "There are the Indians!" Company C however was having other problems at the end of the column. In his recollections later in 1924, Sergeant Kanipe would state that he and Sergeant Finkle were riding together near Captain Tom Custer, their company commander. It was then Finkle's horse began to falter. Likewise riding near the end of Company C and the end of Custer's advancing column, Private Peter Thompson would state in his 1913 recollections that Privates John Brennan and John Fitzgerald, had left the column shortly after visiting the lone teepee. Their horses were giving out. Privates Brennan and Fitzgerald, on their own, turned around and headed back to the pack-train to get fresher mounts. Private Thompson and his friend Private James Watson, together with Privates Brennan and Fitzgerald, formed a "four" in Company C. Companies in action in those days would have the troopers numbered as ones, twos, threes, and fours. The fours were the designated horse holders of all four when the command to dismount and form skirmish line was given. The fours were usually the most senior of the groupings, as they had the most experience with the horses.

The ones, twos, and threes would move a few paces forward of the horse-holder fours. At a lateral separated distance of about five yard increments per the Army Cavalry manual, these troopers would form the dismounted skirmish line.

As Company C began to climb the high ground up the bluffs from Reno Creek, Privates Thompson and Watson began to experience problems with their mounts. Thus Company C at the rear of Custer's column was seeing problems with the mounts of at least five troopers of the company's forty odd men and mounts.

Custer sent his remaining Ree and Crow scouts to advance up the bluffs and determine the threats in that direction and the exact location of the village. As the Rees went up the bluffs, Custer watched to his chagrin as they turned left on the bluff tops and then disappeared to the valley below. Three of the Crow scouts continued north along the high bluffs overlooking the peaceful camp along the river banks below. Custer would now have to move out himself to see what was going on in the valley and where and how he would attack the village.

Four miles to the southeast, Captain Benteen was having his own difficulties. The bluffs were proving to be very rough terrain to traverse. He had sent his Company H subordinate, Lieutenant Gibson, and a detachment of troopers to ride out front and to scale the high ground as Custer had directed with his last message from Sergeant Major Sharrow. But to gain the needed intelligence of what was in front of his column,

Captain Benteen himself rode about 600 yards in advance of his column. Since his Company H was the lead company and no officer was leading it now, Benteen had Captain Thomas Weir, commander of the second company in line, Company D, lead the column. Captain Weir was a senior captain in the regiment. He had been with Custer and Benteen at the Battle of the Washita. Weir was now acting as Benteen's second-in-command of the column as they pushed forward.

Benteen soon learned from Lieutenant Gibson and his scouting detachment, that the terrain before the column was mostly impassable. Captain Benteen, knowing that Indians would not have a large village in such inhospitable terrain, decided to change direction and head back to Reno Creek. He wanted to find Custer's trail. As they made their way north, they found the watering hole, or morass as it was also known, that Custer had visited not too long before. Benteen let his column water the horses and rest the men for fifteen minutes. He later recalled this at the Reno Court of Inquiry. As they were readying to leave the morass, the pack-train and Captain McDougall's command could be seen approaching on their right, from the east along Reno Creek. A few of the mules broke loose and ran for the water of the morass.

Major Reno's column struck the ford across the Little Bighorn about two and a half miles from where he left Custer's column. Reno ordered his column across the river by column of fours. This was to reduce the time to reassemble his command on the other side.

About this time, the small band of Indians under Little Wolf was between Reno and the southern edge of the Indian village. Little Wolf, sensing the danger, had his warriors find brush and attach it to their ponies' tails. This was to be used to make dust clouds. It was to become a kind of smoke screen to mask the village from the approaching soldiers. Little Wolf then sent word to the quiet village ahead of the impending danger from the soldiers.

Lieutenant Cooke and Captain Keogh observed the crossing by Reno with increased interest. Scout Fred Girard and Captain Moylan of Company A both let Cooke and Keogh know that the village was not running away. Rather, the Indians were preparing to attack Reno. Custer would need to know this immediately. Lieutenant Wallace, riding with the trailing Company G watched as Lieutenant Cooke and Captain Keogh left the ford. The junction of Reno Creek and the Little Bighorn River would later be known as Ford A on Lieutenant Maguire's famous survey map of the battlefield. A rise on the right or east bank of the river near this ford headed up to the high bluffs above the river to the north.

In a draw near the river, Curly, the Crow scout, and the Rees with him found a gathering party of Sioux squaws. The Rees, seeing they were from their tribal enemies, killed ten of the party. Curly found one attractive Sioux whom he bound by the hands. Curly then set off on his pony, dragging this Sioux squaw across the river for his own pleasure. The Rees did not know it, but they and Curly had killed the family of Hunkpapa Chief Gall. Gall would later recall how he heard of the death of his wives early in the fight and fought throughout the day with "a bad heart," an angry, vengeful heart.

As Reno gathered his troops across the Little Bighorn, he formed his attack grouping. He started with Captain Moylan's Company A in column on the right and Captain French's Company M on the left. Lieutenant McIntosh's Company G was in column at the rear. As they moved forward at a trot, Reno had the column formations change. They were ordered to form by line to their left. As the troopers spread to the left to form a long line to face the village, Reno ordered Lieutenant McIntosh to advance his company and extend the long line of troopers to the left. Though the dust cloud made by Little Wolf's band was significant, it could not hide the immensity of the Indian village before Reno's line.

Reno ordered the line forward at a gallop. The young troopers began to wildly shoot their carbines and revolvers in the air even though the village was still out of range. After a two-mile advance, Reno ordered his column to halt. They formed a skirmish line on foot. As the troopers were not well trained in the practice of shooting while mounted, the battle would start on foot. The line advanced on foot another seventy-five yards or so. The time was about 2:30 p.m.

The village was huge, being made up of seven large tribal circles of lodges. The southernmost circle, directly in front of Reno, belonged to the Hunkpapa Sioux of Sitting Bull and Gall. Next were the camps of the Brules, Blackfeet, and Two Kettles Sioux. The Minneconjou and Santee camps were close by. To the north end of the large village were the Oglalas of Crazy Horse, and to the far northern end, the Northern Cheyenne camp of Two Moons. The village extended almost three and a half miles from south to north. In Gall's camp was Inkpaduta, the very same who had eluded soldiers those many years since the Minnesota uprising.

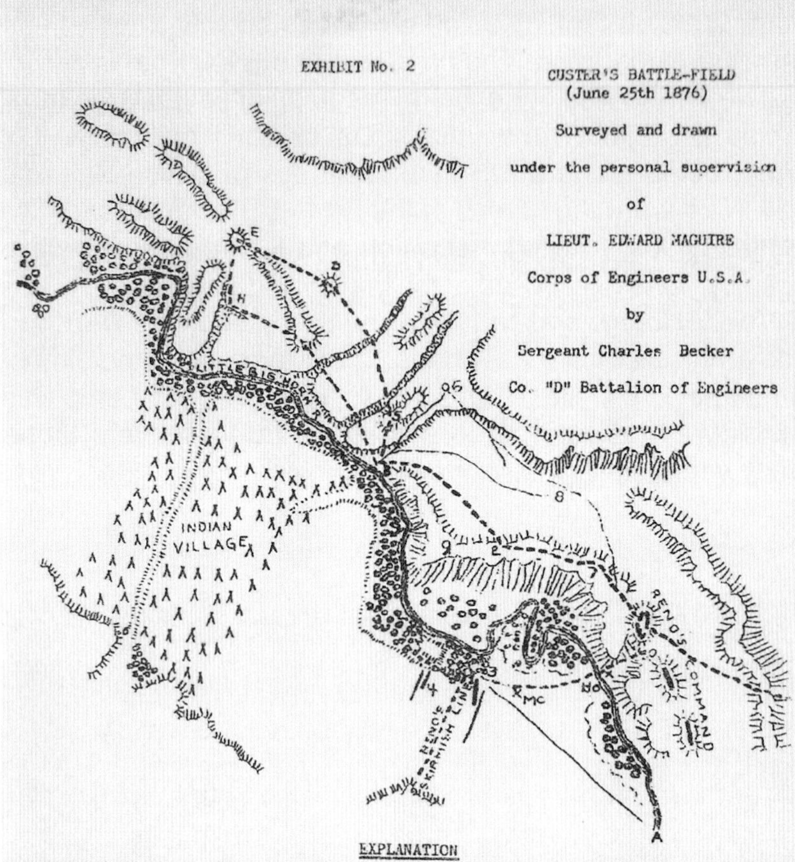

EXPLANATION

A. Reno's crossing and advance down valley.
B. The ford Custer was believed to have tried.
D. Calhoun's stand.
E. Custer Hill, scene of the last stand.
H. Many bodies found here.
Mc. Lt. McIntosh killed here. Marked with X.
Ho. Lt. Hodgson killed here. Marked with X.
1. Girard marks point where he encouraged Reynolds, the Scout.
2. Girard estimates Custer's position when Reno reached hill in retreat.
3. Girard marks point where Reynolds was killed.
4. Herendeen marks point where he dismounted.
5. Hare's estimate of Reno's position, in his advance toward Custer.
6. Hare's estimate of Weir's advance point.
7. DeRudio's estimate of where he saw Custer, during the valley fight.
8. Martin marks point from which he was sent back with message to Benteen to "Come on and be quick".
9. Edgerly's estimate of point of Reno's advance.

Note: The four lines to front and rear of the dotted line on the original map marked "Reno's Skirmish Line", were marked in pencil by witnesses who thought the map incorrectly placed the skirmish line.

-558-

As Reno's troops dismounted, Custer's column came to a high hill on the bluff. This hill would later be known as Sharpshooter Ridge. Custer halted the column on the rise as many things were happening now. Behind him he could see Captain Yates leading his detachment of Companies F and E. Yates was bringing word to Custer that the lone teepee had been burned and destroyed. Sergeant Kanipe and Private Thompson witnessed the return of Captain Yates and his column.

Along the bluffs, Custer saw Captain Keogh and Lieutenant Cooke approaching at a gallop from the direction of Reno's river crossing. Keogh's column was now led by Lieutenant Porter and Company I, followed by Lieutenant Calhoun's Company L, and Captain Tom Custer's Company C. General Custer had Captain Yates pull his column up parallel, to the left of the Keogh column and halt. This put the Yates column closest to Custer and closest to the river along the high bluff. Custer could now better communicate with the two battalions at the same time.

As Captain Keogh and Lieutenant Cooke approached, Custer led them to a spot overlooking the valley below. Together they observed Reno's skirmish line now shooting at the village. This spot in 1992 had a marble marker for modern-day visitors to see the valley below as Custer would have viewed it. The time was about 2:35 p.m. Keogh and Cooke gave Custer the intelligence that Reno had crossed the river without incident. They told him that the scouts reported the Indians were not running away, but were turning to fight.

From the valley below, Lieutenant DeRudio, riding with Company A could see General Custer, Cooke, and "one other" watching the Reno fight from above. Lieutenant DeRudio was in the timber with five or six men of Company A on the "right side," or east side, of the creek. He and Sergeant Davern, who was also in the valley fight, both saw Custer and two other men on the high bluff observing the valley fight. Per Sergeant Davern's testimony at the Reno Court of Inquiry, he "recognized General Custer and Lieutenant Cooke by their dress. They had on blue shirts and buckskin pants" and "by recognizing their peculiar dress" he could identify them. "He (General Custer) and Lieutenant Cooke were the only ones who had blue shirts, and no jacket, and buckskin pants, and besides Lieutenant Cooke had an immense beard (sideburns) which could be recognized at that distance." Per Sergeant Davern, General Custer, Cooke, and Keogh remained and watched for only a minute or so. The three officers waved their hats to the troops below so as to rally them on.

Custer gleened other key intelligence from this view of the Reno fight. The skirmish fighting was only now beginning in the valley below. When Lieutenant Wallace who was riding with Company G in the Reno column crossed the river at Ford A, he looked at his watch and noted it was 2:20 p.m. When Reno's line dismounted and formed the skirmish line, it was 2:30 p.m. In other words, it took ten minutes for the troops to get from Reno Creek to where Custer was. This was roughly two to two and a half miles from the crossing. It took those same ten minutes for Reno to charge and then form his first skirmish line.

From this first high ground, Custer could see Reno was engaging the extreme southern end of the village. Hence, Captain Benteen's column was too far south. Custer would need to recall Benteen to have him participate in attacking the village from a different direction. Based on the time from when Custer had last seen Benteen's column, their gait, and approximate direction, Custer probably knew that Benteen was maybe forty-five minutes to an hour south of this current position overlooking Reno.

The initiative still seemed to be with Custer and his troops. Perhaps by 3:30 p.m. Custer might have his entire regiment in action. He would need Major Reno and his men to hold the Indians in their front for at least another hour in Custer's calculations.

As General Custer, Lieutenant Cooke, and Captain Keogh returned to Sharpshooter Ridge new orders were being issued to the command. The time was about 2:40 p.m.

Custer could see from this current hill, a still higher hill lay farther north. This would make for probably his best view of the whole Indian camp. He still could not see the far north end of the camp. He instructed Captain Yates to have his battalion ride parallel with Captain Keogh's. He informed Captains Keogh, Yates, and Tom Custer, of the need to recall Benteen.

He instructed Captain Custer to send a messenger, a sergeant, from his company back to Benteen to hurry up and rejoin Custer's column. The message instructed Captain McDougall to hurry the pack-train by "coming straight over the plains", rather than following Custer's circuitous trail to Sharpshooter Ridge.

As Captain Custer went back to his company he was looking for Sergeant Finkle to carry the message to Benteen. But as Sergeant Kanipe recalled in 1924, Sergeant Finkle's horse was faltering and falling behind. Captain Custer seeing Sergeant Kanipe close at hand, verbally gave the orders:

"Tell McDougall to bring the pack-train straight across the high ground -if the packs get loose don't stop to fix them, cut them off. Come quick, big camp!".

As Sergeant Kanipe would recount in his later years,

"Away off in the distance, the dust rolling up like a little cloud, I saw the pack-train. I went toward that. My company (C) went on down towards the Indian camp. I remember the last words that I heard General Custer say; the men were on the hill (Sharpshooter Ridge), and we all gave them three cheers riding at a full gallop, some of them couldn't hold their horses, galloping past General Custer. He shouted at them, 'Boys, hold your horses, there are plenty of them down there for us all.' They rode on. I rode back."

For one faltering horse, fate had delivered Daniel Kanipe from the maelstrom that would soon follow. Within the next two hours Sergeant Finkle would lie dead filled with arrows, lying by his dead horse, Carlo.

General Custer's column began to proceed to the next and highest hill (Weir Point) along the bluffs. The men cheered for Custer. As the column headed out, at the rear of Company C two more horses were faltering. Privates Peter Thompson and James Watson were stopped as they watched the column move ahead. Thompson's horse was "down." Watson's horse was "slowed to a walk." The two privates began to walk in the direction of that highest hill. For two more faltering horses, two more men of Company C would be spared their lives. They would live to tell their story of surviving the Battle of the Little Bighorn.

Below in the valley, the first battle of the Little Bighorn was beginning to evolve. As the initial surprise of Reno's daring charge began to fade, the village had by now been alerted. Indian warriors were fast grabbing their repeating rifles, bows, arrows, and war clubs. From the vast pony herd, Indians with the herd were bringing ponies to the warriors in camp. Soon hundreds of warriors were on horseback and advancing toward Reno's skirmish line of ninety men, with thirty others holding their horses.

Still more warriors had crossed to the east bank, the right bank of the river as the soldiers would later recall. These warriors began to provide enfilade fire into Reno's skirmish line. Reno, seeing this danger, went to his left and instructed Lieutenant McIntosh to take a platoon of his Company G and move to their right. They were to gain a spot in the timber near the river to stop this Indian movement.

As Company G split, the mounted Indians continued to move around the extreme open left of Reno's skirmish line. Lieutenant Varnum's Indian scouts had now been turned. The scouts then joined the desperate fight which was beginning to envelop the troopers. The line began to bend on the left. The troopers began to seek refuge in a low area along the river protected by thick timber. The skirmish line had held for fifteen minutes.

As the troopers sought cover, a few took notice of movement high on the bluffs across the river. Within the relatively primitve protection of the timber some of the men saw the gray horse company move out at a gallop. No other men of Custer's column could be seen at that moment. But Lieutenant

DeRudio with Company A, Lieutenant Hare and Fred Girard of the scouts, and Sergeants Davern and Culbertson all testified at the Reno Court of Inquiry as to seeing Custer's column, the "gray horse" company in particular, on the bluff. Only the famous gray horses and their riders of Lieutenant Algernon Smith's Company E were seen during this time and no other. It was assumed that the rest of the command was behind the bluff. They were heading north to attack the village from farther downstream.

Company A nearest the timber at the start of the battle was doing best in this valley fight. However, Company G had already changed face and were now facing west instead of the north. Next to it, Company M and Captain French began to retreat into the timber to avoid the hail of bullets being offered up by the ever increasing numbers of Indians. Captain French was giving instruction to one of his men when that man received a bullet to the back of the head. Captain French yelled out to Major Reno that they were being surrounded. The time was about 3:00 p.m.

About this same time, around 3:00 p.m., Sergeant Kanipe found the pack-train four miles away and delivered his message to Captain McDougall. He then rode forward to Captain Benteen and delivered the same message. Captain Benteen was starting to move forward along Reno Creek.

About twenty minutes later, about 3:20 p.m., another message came from Custer. Benteen decided to ride forward himself to check the Reno ford area. It was here Benteen saw the last of Reno's skirmish line retreating into the timber. He judged by these actions that the whole of Custer's attack had failed. The regiment was in full retreat. The time now was about 3:35 p.m.

Benteen directed his battalion to move up the bluff line. He soon spotted Indians in that direction. They turned out to be the Crow scouts from Custer's column. The time was about 3:45 p.m.

Reno's men were doing what they could to hold on. But even the timber was becoming to hot too defend. Reno, in what some thought a scared or frightened moment, ordered a retreat from the timber to the high ground across the river. As Reno preferred to call the movement at his Court of Inquiry, it was an advance, a charge to the rear. This was to avoid being wiped out by the ever increasing numbers of Indians getting in the column's rear. The charge to the rear took place about fifty-five minutes after the first skirmish line had been formed. Custer needed them to hold for sixty minutes. Reno's retreat occurred about 3:25 p.m.

The Reno charge to the rear lasted about ten minutes. The Indians in their aging memories when interviewed years later, would recall the retreat looking like a great buffalo hunt. The Indians on all sides of the column, shooting and pulling soldiers from their mounts as they jumped into the cold waters of the Little Bighorn. The men of Reno's ragged column of fours desperately rode their horses up the steep ravines leading to the high ground across the river. Custer had vacated the same high ground forty or so minutes before. Panic and fear had become the new weapon in the Indians' arsenal.

As the tired and panicked men of Reno's command reached the heights, they were relieved to be greeted by the approaching column of Captain Benteen. Benteen reached Reno's men about 3:50 p.m. Benteen quickly restored order by deploying his fresh troops and instilling in Reno's tired and battle weary troops a new sense of hope. This essentially ended the first battle of the Little Bighorn.

As the troops of the now combined columns of Reno and Benteen waited for Captain McDougall and the pack-train to arrive, the Indians in the valley for the most part started to depart and head north. Some stayed behind, killing and mutilating the wounded and dead of Reno's command left in the valley below.

Hiding in the thick valley underbrush, were Lieutenant DeRudio, scout Fred Girard, and about twenty others who had not heard the order to retreat. They missed the charge to the high ground. These men would wait quietly in the underbrush until dark or until relieved by the separated columns. Fred Girard told Lieutenants DeRudio and Hare that they might remain here and find Custer's men. This after Custer had advanced south through the village from some northern ford.

As Captain Benteen rode into the disarray of Major Reno's command, Major Reno gave an order, but more in the way of a plea, asking Benteen to halt and regroup with Major Reno's column. Reno, seeing that the Indian pressure from below in the valley was receding, decided to go down the bluff on foot with a small detachment. He wanted to retrieve the body of his young adjutant, Lieutenant Benny Hodgson. Meanwhile Captain Moylan of Company A was in charge of the many wounded who had made it to the top of the bluff. The column's Dr. DeWolfe had been killed as he tried desperately to scale the ravines leading to Reno's position. Dr. Porter, riding with Major Reno's column, hurriedly triaged the wounded as best he could.

About forty-five minutes after Benteen and his men had joined Reno's command, the pack-train with Captain McDougall's Company B arrived. With him he had the additional eighty-four men assigned to Lieutenant Edward Mathey, McDougall's second-in-command. There were 24,000 rounds of ammunition with the packs and Reno's men needed to be replenished.

All during this activity, Captain Thomas Weir, knowing of the last message Custer had sent to Captain Benteen to bring the packs and be quick about it, grew anxious. Major Reno had ordered Benteen to halt and assist Reno's command. Custer had ordered Benteen to rush to the north and join Custer. As the confusion on the hill, the Reno-Benteen Hill as it would be known, persisted, Captain Weir made a decision to advance his Company D. He wanted to find Custer. Captain Weir had long been with Custer and the 7th Cavalry. He had been at the Battle of the Washita, with his company commander, Captain Louis McLane Hamilton. Captain Hamilton, a grandson to Alexander Hamilton, was shot from his saddle and killed during the attack. Custer had promoted

Weir to command the company on the spot. Captain Weir, a brevet lieutenant- colonel during the Civil War, knew that Custer would be looking for Benteen's column. Benteen was now long overdue in following Custer's order.

Captain Weir mounted up his Company D and slowly started north along the high bluff. In his front he could see a high hill from which he might gain a view of Custer's position. As he began the one and a half mile trek, slowly other companies began to mount up and follow Weir. Captain Moylan and Company A were detailed to transport the wounded. Six men were assigned to carry each wounded trooper as they moved forward.

The caravan moved slowly and in a long file. When reaching the high ground, now known as Weir Point, Captain Weir made a study of the dust cloud off in the distance. He halted his company slightly beyond the high hill. Captain Benteen and his Company H occupied the highest part of the hill. Captain Benteen would later testify at the Reno Court of Inquiry, that from this hill alone, could the whole of the large Indian village be seen. To Benteen's right he deployed Captain French's Company M. Next to them was Lieutenant Wallace and the small remnants of Company G. And, to their right, Lieutenant Godfrey's Company K formed a line. In this manner on the high ridge they made a visible show of the command's position to a hopefully searching Custer.

They never did see Custer or his men. Rather they observed a slow procession of mounted Indians shooting at objects on the ground. Lieutenant Varnum with the scouts, observed on this high hill next to Benteen a small stack of rocks and some medicine pouches. Little did he know that these were the same items which Sitting Bull had left the evening before.

As the soldiers slowly began to gather on these heights, they were taken aback by a large charging force of hundreds of Indians. Arising from the lower depths of Medicine Tail Coulee, the on-rushing sight must have frightened even the most battle hardened of troopers. Now began the short second battle of the southern Little Bighorn Battlefield.

Captain Benteen, quickly judging that the column was in open ground and vastly outnumbered, gave orders to Captain French and Lieutenant Godfrey to establish a skirmish line to slow the Indians. While these companies began a covering fire, Captain Benteen and Major Reno ordered the column to reverse direction and set up a defensive perimeter on the ground they had recently vacated. It seemed to offer the best protection in the judgment of Reno and Benteen.

As the column of companies regained their position on the Reno-Benteen Hill, Benteen set his Company H at the most southern and exposed position. Captain Moylan's Company A faced southeast to the left of Benteen. Company B faced west overlooking the Little Bighorn Valley on the right of Benteen. Captain Weir and his Company D faced the open ground to the east.

Lieutenant Wallace and only three active Company G troopers held a large gap between Captain Weir's Company D and Captain Moylan's Company A. As the companies of Captain French and Lieutenant Godfrey began a slow fighting retreat, Captain French relayed orders to Godfrey that Company K should fight on foot and fire to cover Company M's retreat. Lieutenant Edward Godfrey stood with his men as they fired volley after volley until they too were in the concentrated circle of defense setup by Captain Benteen and Major Reno.

The advancing Indians soon took up positions in the hills and ravines surrounding the Reno-Benteen defensive circle. This ended the short, but eventful, second of the southern Little Bighorn battles.

Then firing from afar began. The trek to and from Weir Point had lasted a little more than an hour. They had left a little after 5:00 p.m. and had returned sometime around 6:00 p.m. But the third and last battle of the southern battles would be the longest. The men were tired, thirsty, and hot. As the hundreds of Indians around them continued to pour fire into the ring of soldiers, the soldiers laid low and returned fire.

The mules of the pack-train and the wounded under Dr. Porter's care, were concentrated in a low swale in the center of the troops. Still, without timber or other cover, the bullets from the Indians continued to inflict damage on the men, mules, and horses. They remained exposed. From 6:00 p.m. until the end of daylight around 9:45 p.m., the Indians kept up their fire from all directions. As darkness settled in, the firing slowed. Benteen and Reno gave orders for the men to dig rifle pits. They were to stack any boxes or packs they could for a better cover when the new day would begin on the 26th.

Trenching tools were few. The men scraped the hard Montana soil with their knives, their tin cups, with their bare hands -anything to gain a few inches of cover. As the night grew quiet, many then took whatever sleep they could. Many wondered what had become of Custer and his troops. Where were they? When would they come and rejoin these troops? Where was General Terry and Colonel Gibbon's column? What would tomorrow bring as the sun returned to light up the surrounding countryside?

Those who hid in the thick brush below the hill made their plans for escape as well. The darkness would provide cover, so some crawled their way into the Little Bighorn River and swam to the otherside. A few troopers in the timber on the right bank found ravines that would bring them to Reno's last spotted position. Still others would wait until early light and then make their move, either up the bluffs or back down the river to the original ford.

By sundown on the 25th, General Terry and his men were still twenty-five to thirty miles to the north. The marches had been brutally slow. The mouth of the Little Bighorn River still lay a good day's march in front of them. More disturbing, the advanced elements of Major Brisbin's 2nd Cavalry had run into hostile Indians wearing cavalry uniforms. They were even riding in cavalry-like formations. Most unsettling of all, early on the morning of the 26th, three Crow scouts known to be riding with Custer had said that he and all his men were dead. The interpreters asked four times the meaning of these words from the Crow scouts. The Crows insisted that they were true.

The day of the 26th started as the previous day had ended for Major Reno and Captain Benteen. The Indians were close by on all sides. The bullets were finding their mark and taking a toll on the prone soldiers. So too was the rising sun and the dry heat. On Benteen's front the Indians were within a stone's throw of overrunning the troops. Captain Benteen, with utmost focus, organized a desperate trooper charge to shock the hostiles immediately over the ridge. The charge caught the Indians off guard and they hastily retreated. Benteen lost one man in the charge.

With most canteens now empty from the previous day's hard ride and battles, the cries for water began to become more prevalent. Especially hard to endure were the feeble cries of the more seriously wounded. Dr. Porter advised Reno and Benteen that many would die if they did not get water. A plan was devised to send a detail to fill canteens. Four men were selected to provide cover fire while fifteen others found their way down a steep ravine to the Little Bighorn River below. Only one of the water carriers was wounded in the leg during the dash back: Private Mike Madden of Company K. The fifteen water carriers and the four sharpshooters were later awarded Congressional Medals of Honor. One of these was Private Peter Thompson, from Company C, the one and same whose horse faltered along the Custer column's trail.

The third and final battle of the southern battles was one of Indian sharpshooters trying to hit troopers. The troopers fired back from their defensive circle. One Indian on a high hill, later to be designated Sharpshooters Ridge, was taking careful aim at troopers of M Company. He had located a line of blue targets. First Sergeant John Ryan of M Company described the action,

"There was a high ridge on the right (north) . . . one Indian in particular I must give credit for being a good shot. . . .While we were lying in line he fired a shot and killed the fourth man on my right. Soon afterward he fired again and shot the third man. His third shot wounded the man next to my right, who jumped back from the line, and down among the rest of the wounded. I thought my turn was coming next. I jumped up, with Captain French, and some half a dozen members of my company, and instead of firing straight to the front, as we had been doing . . . we wheeled to our right and put in a deadly volley, and I think we put an end to that Indian, as there were no more men killed in that particular spot."

By 6:00 p.m. that evening of the 26th, something remarkable happened. The large village of thousands of Indians began to move off to the south. To the soldiers, the Indians looked like one large brown mass, nearly a mile wide and three miles in length. The procession moved steadily into the waning light of the late evening. That night the last of the stragglers from the valley fight made it up the bluffs and rejoined the command.

The next morning on the 27th, the slow moving column of General Terry finally made it to Reno's defensive circle. The men on the hill welled up with tears of joy and relief. Their battle was done. But they all asked Terry, where was Custer and his men? General Terry from the news brought to him by the three Crow scouts, and confirmed by lead elements of his cavalry, found the answer to the question. Lying motionless, stripped bare of uniforms, and amongst the dead of their mounts, Custer's columns had been overrun and killed to the man. Terry's search parties had yielded no surviving souls to tell their tale. The confusion and accusations of the day were only beginning to be told, as emotions and guilt ran high.

Thus ended the third battle of the southern battles. This was this the final battle of the Battle of the Little Bighorn. But what really happened to the men who followed Custer?

6

The Battle at Ford B, a Fateful Turn

What happened to Lieutenant- Colonel, brevet Major General, George Armstrong Custer and his men? Two primary stories evolved into the accepted tale of Custer's final battle. One was the story as told by Custer's Crow scout, Curly. The other story evolved from the battlefield survey and burial detail as the Terry column prepared to exit the battlefields. The reports made within the next few days would soon become newspaper headlines.

Indians would tell their stories of the day, but they began to understand and incur the white man's revenge and retaliation. They began to change their stories over time as the lore of the battle unfolded.

Custer enthusiasts and friends could have George Custer die no less than a hero. Custer detractors would say his rashness and zeal to make headlines would drive him to deadly consequence. Soon white man and Indian had Custer bravely standing with the last of his men on a hill to be known as Last Stand Hill. But what did the survivors understand, and how did their widely differing views of these desperate struggles to the north all make sense together?

The things today that are as they were on that June 25th, are the times of day that the sunrises and sunsets take place. These remain as 5:24 a.m. and 9:08 p.m. local Mountain

Time. The terrain and topography are much the same. True, the Little Bighorn River has changed course in some bends of the river, but the bluffs, the landmarks of 1876 can still be identified in modern times. The use of current topographic maps and aerial mapping photos show exact distances between places referenced in the many testimonies of the surviving participants.

Key to understanding the northern battles are the testimonies of Sergeant Daniel Kanipe and trooper Peter Thompson, both from the trailing company of Company C, and Trumpeter John Martin. Captain Benteen's recollections of his column's scout through the bluff country becomes clear when reading his testimony and following detailed topographic maps.

From the Indian survivors the testimony of surviving warriors added credence to the details found about the dead. In particular the memory of White Cow Bull, later known as Joseph White Cow Bull, and his story as related to the writer David Humphreys Miller in the 1930s stands out in its significance. The Crow scouts, Hairy Moccasin, Goes Ahead, and White Man Runs Him, all added a clear understanding of the first of the northern battles. The interpreters of the time did not clearly understand the detail they offered. Custer himself was the master of interpretation for these Indians. Not until much later when they were interviewed in the early twentieth century, did their accounts add to the clarification needed to understand the fates of Custer's two battalions.

As stated earlier, Custer was seen on the bluffs overlooking the valley fight at about 2:35 p.m. His command was then on the high ground of Sharpshooter Ridge, but out of view by Reno's command below the bluff. When the command had halted on Sharpshooter Ridge, Trumpeter Martin and Sergeant Kanipe both later recalled that the troopers of the command could now see the village for the first time. As Martin stated at the Reno Court of Inquiry:

"All at once we looked on the bottom and saw the Indian village, at the same time we could see only children and dogs and ponies around the village, no Indians at all. General

Custer appeared to be glad to see the village in that shape, and supposed the Indians were asleep in their teepees."

Custer sent his third of four messages to Captain Benteen with Sergeant Kanipe riding to the south. It took twenty minutes, but Sergeant Kanipe found the pack-train and Captain Benteen's column. They were between four and five miles away, along the last few miles of Reno Creek per Benteen's testimony at the Reno Court of Inquiry. Sergeant Kanipe later recalled he could see the dust trail of the pack-train from the "high hill," Sharpshooter Ridge, before he headed back. In other words the McDougall column was in visible range for Custer to see and plan his next moves.

Captain Benteen had given up on his valley hunting and actually was much closer to Custer than Custer had figured. Benteen's column was watering their horses at the morass referenced in Benteen's testimony. Sergeant Kanipe found Benteen shortly after his column left the watering morass on Reno Creek. The initiative still appeared to be in the 7th Cavalry's favor.

It took about five minutes for Custer to reach Weir Point from Sharpshooter Ridge. He decided to ascend the high hill to get a better view of the large village. He took with him his brother, Captain Tom Custer, and probably his nephew, Autie Reed, per Martin's recollections. The time was close to 2:50 p.m. Trumpeter Martin testified that he saw Custer with his brother and his nephew on that "high hill" at the Reno Court of Inquiry. Another Custer brother, Boston Custer, was also with the column. Boston, General Custer's youngest brother, had departed the column back at Sharpshooter Ridge. Boston went back to the pack-train to get a fresher mount.

As the Custer command moved from Sharpshooter Ridge to Weir Point, Private Peter Thompson and Private James Watson at the end of column with Company C, had their horses give out. Thompson later recalled that he and Watson watched as the column disappeared from their view. As the column descended from Sharpshooter Ridge, Custer's column descended a coulee now known as Cedar Coulee.

Privates Thompson and Watson took some time to try and get Thompson's mount back on its feet. As they worked their issues with their tired mounts, Custer continued forward.

The view from Weir Point, as it turned out, was the only high ground from which to see the whole village. Captain Benteen testified at the Reno Court of Inquiry that only from this "highest hill" could the entire extent of the village be seen. He observed this as his column later advanced to this position following Captain Weir's advance.

Sometime between 2:55 p.m. and 3:00 p.m. Custer needed to complete his full reconaissance of the village. He knew Major Reno was heavily engaged on the southern end of the village. The northern end was still two miles to the north. To encircle and strike the village from both ends and the middle, he needed Benteen's column. He also needed the extra ammunition with Captain McDougall and the pack-train. As Custer formed his battle plan in his mind, he reviewed his attack considerations with his senior company commanders, Captains Keogh, Yates, and Captain Custer, and his adjutant Lieutenant William Cooke. Things needed to happen rapidly to be successful. Custer had seen either "sleeping Indians in their teepees," or "skeddadling Indians" as Trumpeter Martin would later recall. These appearances occurred: 1) as Sitting Bull had been feverishly ordering the village to run to the high plains to the west of the village to escape the soldiers' bullets, and 2) while the warriors rushed to the south end of the village to fight off Reno's attack.

The Custer column halted in the low ground before Weir Point while this reconnaisance occurred. Privates Thompson and Watson could not get Thompson's horse to budge. They set off on foot to follow the Custer column.

To strengthen Yates and his battalion, General Custer wanted Captain Custer's Company C currently at the rear of Keogh's battalion, to left oblique march and join the Yates column. This would make Captain Yates' battalion the attack battalion, which Custer would himself lead into the center of the village.

As Custer remounted his horse, Vic, he had the two columns of Keogh and Yates, which were in columns of twos, move to the right and descend Cedar Coulee, looking as a column of fours. Captain Yates with Company F led the left two files, with Lieutenant Algernon Smith's Company E and their gray horses following. The right two files were led by Captain Keogh and his Company I, followed in order by Lieutenant Calhoun's Company L, and then Captain Custer's Company C. This order of companies is significant to understand the following discussion of the northern battles. The gray horse company was seen at the end of the Custer column when Captain Benteen's scout headed southwest. Captain Benteen testified that the last he saw of the Custer column was the gray horse company. When asked at the Reno Court of Inquiry, Trumpeter Martin testified that the gray horse company was in the "middle" of the Custer column. Men from the Reno column in their valley fight testified they saw only the gray horse company along the bluffs.

Trumpeter Martin testified that once at the base of the "high hill", Weir Point, the column took a right turn and went down a ravine away from the Little Bighorn River. This ravine is now known as Cedar Coulee. Martin said the column went all the way down this ravine until it opened to the large Medicine Tail Coulee. Here the column made a left turn. The column was moving at a fast gait per Martin. About a half mile from this last turn Lieutenant Cooke handed Martin a hurriedly written message to be delivered to Captain Benteen:

Benteen, Come On. Big Village. Be quick. Bring packs. W. W. Cooke. ps Bring pack.

To strengthen Yates and his battalion, General Custer wanted Captain Custer's Company C, currently at the rear of Keogh's battalion, to oblique march to the left and join the Yates column. This would put the gray horse company, Company E, in the center of the column. Again, Trumpeter John Martin, when asked where he saw the gray horse company at the Reno Court of Inquiry, replied, "In the center of the column." This was the last close-up view of Custer's column made by a surviving trooper.

The Crow Indian scouts riding with Custer had been dismissed by head scout Mitch Bouyer as the village location was now known. These three Crow Indians decided to stay on the high ground of the bluffs rather than follow Custer's column into the Medicine Tail Coulee. They continued north until they were on the last bluff overlooking the village. From here they could see the sleeping village. They knew though that in the commotion below, the Indians of the village were not running from the fight. Rather they were organizing in heavy numbers for a fight. They could see the only ford, Ford B, the Medicine Tail Coulee Ford, from which Custer would strike the village at its middle.

If Custer was on Weir Point at 3:00 p.m. and left at 3:05 p.m, it took another five minutes to ride down to Medicine Tail Coulee. The time was about 3:10 p.m. Custer probably was planning to launch his attack into the middle of the village at about 3:30 p.m. In this manner he could support Major Reno whose column was now beginning to withdraw into the cover of the timber.Orders had been given to have Captain Benteen's column move north to assist in attacking the north end of the village.

About this same time, Sergeant Kanipe was delivering Captain Custer's verbal orders for Benteen and Captain McDougall's pack-train to hurry to Custer's location. Now even Captain Benteen's column had notice of the battle plan Custer was putting into action. The problem, however, was Captain Benteen did not understand the urgency of Custer's instructions.

Major Reno's valley fight had been going badly. Reno and Captain Moylan from Company A both looked for Custer to support them, "with the whole regiment." They anticipated Custer would support them from the direction from which they came, at Ford A. Lieutenant DeRudio of Company A and scout Fred Girard both saw Custer's column moving north on the bluffs. They figured Custer's men would come in from the north, through the village to relieve Reno's hard-pressed men.

By 3:25 p.m. Reno felt he could no longer hold his position without being wiped out. He panicked and ordered "anyone who wishes to live" to follow him to the high bluffs across the river.

As Privates Thompson and Watson approached the high hill of Weir Point, they were drawn to Indian artifacts and stacked rocks on this high ground. They were most likely Sitting Bull's medicine rocks from the night before. But before they could get to the high hill, they spotted armed Indian warriors on the high ground ahead. Privates Thompson and Watson quickly sought cover down the steep slopes of the high bluffs. They slid quickly to the low ground of the Little Bighorn riverbanks.

At 3:15 p.m, as Thompson and Watson were sliding down the bluff, Trumpeter Martin was riding back along the column's trail, up Cedar Coulee. He was about to turn south along the bluffs. As he looked back he saw a column of cavalry rapidly riding away from the Little Bighorn River valley, actually the Medicine Tail Coulee. He would later think that this was the full retreat of the Custer column. It was not.

As he turned south from Weir Point, the same Indians that had scared off Privates Thompson and Watson took aim at Martin. They managed to hit Martin's horse in its rear flank. As Martin continued south along the bluff, he ran into Boston Custer now on a fresh mount heading north. Boston asked which way to Custer's column and Martin pointed the way. Boston pointed out to Martin that Martin's horse had a fresh wound in its flank. Martin would recall this incidental meeting, but failed to mention it at the Reno Court of Inquiry. When Boston caught up to the Custer column, he would have been asked how far and how long was it from the pack-train. He would have said that not more than four miles, perhaps twenty minutes at a fast trot.

Trumpeter Martin did find Captain Benteen, whose column was now perhaps a mile or two from the Reno ford, Ford A.

Benteen read the note and showed it to his second-in-command Captain Weir. He then put the message in his soldier's blouse. It would not be seen officially again until Benteen produced it at the Reno Court of Inquiry in 1879.

Benteen got the impression from Martin that Custer was attacking the village and the Indians were "skedaddling" before him. Martin's delivery seemed to indicate that all was going well for Custer and his attack. Benteen chose to ride quickly to the river crossing a few minutes ahead of him. He wanted to see what was happening in the river valley as this was where the shooting was being heard by him. It was about 3:25 p.m.

As he got to the Ford A, he watched as Reno's men appeared in retreat from the valley. They were scurrying to the cover of the timber along the river and to the river banks. Benteen later testified that he thought the whole regiment had been engaged here and that Custer had been badly defeated. The flaw in his testimony was that both of General Custer's messengers, Kanipe and Martin, had come from the high bluffs to the right, and not the river valley.

Benteen rode back to his column. He decided not to ride into the valley, but to the high bluffs to the north and right of his column. His column was now coming into view along the last mile of Reno creek.

Back in the Medicine Tail Coulee, after Trumpeter Martin left around 3:05 p.m., Custer must have halted his columns. Since Benteen could not be engaged for at least another thirty or more minutes, that is assuming Benteen followed orders and came quickly, Custer had time available for final orders and a final scout.

With Yates' and his battalion strengthened by CaptainTom Custer's Company C from Keogh's battalion, there was time to rest the men and mounts. Custer himself would make a final scout for a river ford and point of attack. Custer knew that the pack-train would be last to get into the action. Benteen's column would need a rally point as they tried to join Custer. To this end he ordered Captain Keogh to take his Company I and Company L to the top of a large rise immediately to their right, north in this case. This rise would later be known as Nye-Cartwright or Blummer Ridge. Custer probably instructed Captain Keogh, who was now his second-in-command by rank in this part of the battlefield, to make visible a long blue line of his two companies to attract Benteen. Benteen himself used this tactic when trying to let the northern battalions know of Reno's and Benteen's columns presence at the Weir Point fight.

Captain Keogh was probably told of Custer's attack plan by Custer and Lieutenant. Cooke. Captain Keogh was an experienced officer who had long served with the general. Captain Keogh and Lieutenant Cooke were the only other officers at that moment, besides General Custer, who were knowledgable of the deployment of the four attack battalions. They would have had knowledge of their general locations on the battlefield.

General Custer planned to proceed with Captain Yates and his battalion in his attack. They would strike the village center, as had been done at the Washita. As Reno was engaged on the south end of the village, Captain Benteen would proceed north and strike the village at its north end. Captain Keogh would wait for Captain McDougall and the pack train, and then move into the village center. This last move would reinforce Custer and the Yates battalion, and secure the village center. This plan would then force the hostile Indians to settle for a parley and surrender to Long Hair Custer. If the hostiles fought they would suffer many casualties, including women, children and elder Indians.

Custer then told Captain Yates of Company F that he would now have a reinforced battalion consisting of three companies for the imminent attack. Custer himself would lead. But Custer needed one more piece of vital information: where to ford the Little Bighorn River to attack the village center.

As Captain Keogh led his two-company battalion up the ravine to the heights of Nye-Cartwright, Trumpeter Martin approached the high ground just below Weir Point. This was around 3:10 p.m. Trumpeter Martin turned in his saddle to look where he had been and saw a column of cavalry rushing up a high hill. He would in later years wrongfully relate this sighting as the retreat of Custer's and Captain Yates' column from Ford B. On Lieutenant Maguire's map Ford B was the ford where the Medicine Tail Coulee met the Little Bighorn. In reality, from Martin's position below Weir Point, he could not see the ford, nor the nearby Greasy Grass Ridge. The Greasy Grass height was used by Captain Yates in his retreat. Martin was witnessing the movement of Captain Keogh and his battalion of Company I and Lieutenant Calhoun's Company L and their deployment to Nye-Cartwright Ridge.

Boston Custer now rode down Cedar Coulee from the high bluffs to find the General and Captain Yates halted in the Medicine Tail Coulee. The ride which Boston Custer took from the pack-train back on Reno Creek, to where Yates and his men were halted should not have taken more than thirty minutes. The distance covered was a little over five miles. If Boston was at a gallop, it would have been a twenty minute ride. This information would help the general in his final attack planning.

When Sergeant Kanipe found Captain Benteen and delivered the verbal order to advance quickly to Custer with the pack-train, Benteen hestitated. Benteen did not have the pack-train under his command and dismissed the need for urgency. Benteen told Kanipe to find and report to McDougall, farther back along Reno Creek. Captain McDougall, after all, was in command of the pack-train. This was a rather dismissive rebuff to Custer to whom Benteen felt no imperative obligation.

With Keogh heading up to the rise on the right of the halted column, Company C reassigned to Yates and his battalion, Lieutenant Cooke having sent Trumpeter Martin to retrieve Benteen and his column, all seemed to be going well for Custer. With time to rest the Yates battalion horses and time for Benteen to ride north, Custer still hoped to attack the village center at 3:30 p.m.

With the Indians pre-occupied with Reno and his battalion, the village center should remain open. It should have been little defended for an easier assault. Off to Custer's left, he would have seen a gentle rising ravine to the north (right) of Weir Point. The general rode off on his own toward the river on the other side of the bluffs. He was hoping to find a surprise ford for his attack. He wanted to attack somewhere other than the wide open Medicine Tail Coulee ford, which he could see from the halted column's position.

As he crossed over the last high ridge and descended to the flats of the river bank, the general came upon a disturbing sight. His Crow scout, Curly, was riding back from the village across the river. With him was a captured Indian squaw bound at the hands. She was being forcefully led away by the mounted Curly.

At this same time Privates Thompson and Watson had stumbled through the brush escaping the Indians on Weir Point above. They happened to witness Custer and his encounter with Curly.

Thompson would recall the incident many times in his later years, though historians often dismissed it as inconsistent with what was thought of as a constantly moving Custer and his troops. Custer angrily scolded Curly and told him to release his hostage. Curly complied. Custer then pointed Curly to where the column was halted. Curly and his recollections would become the subject of many debates as many white men would interpret and re-interpret Curly's words and sign language. Most likely he turned and rode to the soldiers high on Nye-Cartwright Ridge. Curly did see the battle at Ford B, but his recollections of the fight were from a distance. And as he later survived the day, he did not ride with any of Custer's men to Battle Ridge.

As Custer turned in the saddle, he continued to look for a ford. He saw instead Privates Thompson and Watson in the brush on foot. Custer "waved to them without saying a word" and pointed the direction of the column. With a final look at the deep banks along the river here, Custer determined that the attack would have to be made at the Medicine Tail Coulee, Ford B. He turned his mount, Vic, and went to the Medicine Tail Coulee and then back to the awaiting Yates battalion. As Thompson recalled in a 1913 interview:

"Custer was mounted on his sorrel horse and it being a very hot day he was in his shirt sleeves, his buckskin pants tucked in his boots, his buckskin shirt fastened to the rear of his saddle, and a broad brimmed cream colored hat on his head, the brim of which was turned up on the right side and fastened to a small hook and eye and to its crown. This gave him the opportunity to sight in his rifle while riding. His rifle lay horizontally in front of him, while riding he leaned slightly forward. This was the appearance of Custer on the day he entered into his last battle."

Thompson spoke of the meeting between Custer and the Crow Indian scout and the Indian woman hostage:

> ***Coming out of the river was one of our Crow scouts, mounted on his horse with a rawhide rope over his shoulder, which he held firmly in his right hand. At the other end of the rope, straining and tugging to get away, was a Sioux squaw. The rope was tied around both her hands, but, struggle as she might, she could not break away. While looking on and wondering where the Crow was going we were further astonished by seeing General Custer dash out of the fording place and ride up rapidly to the Crow and commence to talk to him. Custer was well versed in several Indian languages. The conversation with the Indian did not last long, and what the nature was I do not know, but the Crow released the Sioux woman, and she seemed to be glad to be free came running towards us (Privates Thompson and Watson) in a half stooping posture and in her hand was a***

> ***long bladed knife of ugly dimensions. So fierce did she look that my hand involuntarily sought the handle of my revolver. She must have noticed the movement for she made a short circle around us, ran over the bank, crossed the river, and disappeared in the village. . . . When the Crow scout left him, he (Custer) wheeled around and made for the same point in the river where we had first seen him. While he was passing us he slightly checked his horse and waved his right hand twice for us to follow him. He pointed downstream (north), put spurs to his horse and disappeared at the ford, never uttering a word. This was the last I ever saw of Custer alive. He must have gone thence directly to his command. We wondered why none of his staff were with him. . . . His being alone shows with what fearlessness he travelled about even in an enemy's country with hostiles all around him.***

The time was about 3:20 p.m. Thompson and Watson watched the general disappear. They decided to follow the river banks in the brush further north. They anticipated running into Custer's column somewhere near there.

As Custer returned to Captain Yates and his battalion it was about 3:25 p.m. He gave the order to mount up and move forward with his attack. He moved the gray horse company, Company E, to a parallel position on the left of Capt. Yates' Company F. Looking as a column of fours, in reality, the two companies were in columns of twos, with Company C following. This formation would shorten the column's length, and put both Captain Yates and Lieutenant Smith near the front of the attack to receive battle instructions as soon as they forded the river.

At 3:25 p.m. two and a half miles to the south, Major Reno was now in full retreat from the valley seeking relief on the high bluffs. Minutes before Trumpeter Martin had passed this spot on his way south to find Benteen. And about this time

Benteen received Martin and his message. Benteen was along Reno Creek a mile or so from where Reno had forded the river, an hour before. Benteen decided to ride in advance of his column and go to the ford in his front. Orders from General Custer wanted him to proceed north with his column. Captain Weir of Company D was in advance of Benteen's column a short distance behind on Reno Creek.

In the village, already in commotion due to Reno's sudden attack, much was going on. Many Indians from the seven large camps had ridden south to fight off the soldiers on that end of the village. Chief Gall of the Hunkpapas was rallying the braves and fighting off these soldiers. Sometime late during this fight, an Indian squaw soaking wet from crossing the river found Gall. She told him of how she had escaped a Crow and survived a terrible attack by Rees and this Crow. During this attack they had killed ten Indian squaws, among them Gall's family. Gall's family had been brutally killed while he was fighting off Reno's troops. Gall would in later years say his heart turned angry and vengeful at that moment. He killed soldiers with his bare hands, armed only with knife and warclub.

Near Ford B, White Cow Bull had spent a peaceful morning. He was an Oglala and the Oglala camp was across the river ford. Crazy Horse's Oglala and the Northern Cheyenne of Two Moons were camped to the north. White Cow Bull recalled in 1937 and again in 1938 to David Humphreys Miller that the Oglalas had slept in late that day. They had celebrated a scalp dance late into the previous night. White Cow Bull had gotten up to look for an Indian woman whom he had tried to court. Her name was Monahseetah. She had returned moments before from the river with her young son Yellow Bird after gathering morning firewood. They greeted each other when White Cow Bull found his Cheyenne friend Roan Bear. They talked of the great brave deeds they had performed the week before on the Rosebud in defeating General Crook. They were joined by another Cheyenne, Bobtail Horse.

At that moment an old Cheyenne elder named Mad Wolf found them. He pointed across the river. Approaching were soldiers coming down the coulee. Five Sioux were running for their lives in front of the approaching column. Another Cheyenne warrior, White Shield, joined White Cow Bull and this small band. These ten warriors decided to make a fight of it at the river crossing.

Across the river on the last high bluff, the three Crow scouts who had led Custer to the Little Bighorn -Hairy Moccasin, Goes Ahead, and White Man Runs Him -dismounted from their ponies. They began firing their rifles at the ten defenders below. They anxiously watched as Long Hair Custer led his soldiers down this coulee and to their fate. They were astonished at what they saw next.

At 3:30 p.m. Custer hesitated at first along the river bank assessing the Indian resistance in his front. Then he began to cross the river. Bobtail Horse had an old single-shot muzzleloader. He fired at a soldier on a gray horse. The soldier fell from his mount, the first casualty of the battle at Ford B. This soldier on a gray horse, next to a soldier carrying a flag on a gray horse, per White Cow Bull, fell into the river. This first casualty was most likely First Lieutenant Algernon Smith, leading Company E. Wounded but not dead, Lieutenant Smith would be retrieved by Captain Yates and the battalion as the battalion provided cover fire.

White Cow Bull, who had a repeater rifle (either a Henry or Winchester) quickly returned a few shots at the Crows firing from the heights on the right above the river. Per White Cow Bull:

> ***I looked across the ford and saw that the soldiers had stopped at the edge of the river. I had never seen white soldiers before, so I remember thinking how pink they looked. One white man had little hairs on his face and was wearing a big hat and a buckskin jacket. He was riding fine looking big horse, a sorrel with a blazed face and four***

white stockings. On one side of him was a soldier carrying a flag and riding a gray horse, and on the other was a small man on a dark horse. This small man didn't look much like a white man to me, so I gave the man in the buckskin jacket my attention. He was looking straight at us across the river. Bobtail Horse told us to stay hidden so this man couldn't see how few of us there really were. The man in the buckskin jacket seemed to be the leader of these soldiers, for he shouted something and they all came charging at us across the ford. Bobtail Horse fired first, and I saw a soldier on a gray horse (not the flag carrier) fall out of his saddle into the water. The other soldiers were shooting at us now. The man who seemed to be the soldier chief was firing his heavy rifle fast. I aimed my repeater at him and fired. I saw him fall out of his saddle and hit the water. Shooting that man stopped the soldiers from charging on. They all raised up and gathered around where he had fallen. I fired again, aiming this time at the soldier with the flag. I saw him go down as another soldier grabbed the flag out of his hands. By this time the air was getting thick with gunsmoke and it was hard to see just what happened. The soldiers were firing again and again, so we were kept busy dodging bullets that kicked up dust all around. When it cleared a little, I saw the soldiers do a strange thing. Some of them got off their horses in the ford and seemed to be dragging something out of the water, while the other soldiers still on horseback kept shooting at us. Suddenly we heard war cries behind us. I looked back and saw hundreds of Lakotas (Sioux) and Shahiyela (Cheyenne) warriors charging toward us. They must have driven away those other soldiers who had attacked the Hunkpapa camp circle

and were racing to us to drive off these attackers. The soldiers must have seen them too, for they fell back to the far bank, and those still on horseback got off to fight on foot. As warriors rode up to join us at the ridge a big cry went up.

Per White Cow Bull's narrative to David Humphreys Miller, it becomes clear as to the short but decisive fight at Ford B. Custer was leading, in White Cow Bull's narrative, with a buckskin jacket on. Either Custer put the buckskin jacket on after his encounter with Privates Thompson and Watson, or the translation of White Cow Bull's words could have meant "buckskins" and referred only to the buckskin pants Custer wore, as per Thompson's description. Thompson's description matches that seen earlier by Lieutenant DeRudio. DeRudio described Custer's uniform similarly when he had seen Custer fifty minutes earlier on the high bluffs watching Reno's engagement. The horse with the blazed face and white socks matched only one horse that day, Vic, Custer's mount going into battle.

The time was 3:35 p.m. Privates Thompson and Watson were coming into view of the battle at the ford. They had briefly tried to cross the river upstrem of the ford, thinking that Reno's men might be in the village by now. But they encountered warriors in ever increasing numbers. Then as he recalled in his narrative:

We had scarcely been concealed ten minutes before we heard a heavy volley of rifle shots down the stream (at the ford), followed by a scattering fire. I raised to my feet and parting the brush with my gun; the stalks being covered with long sharp thorns, which made it quite disagreeable for a person's clothes and flesh. Looking through this opening down the stream, I could see Custer's command drawn up in battle line, two men deep in a half circle facing the Indians who were crossing

> ***the river both above and below them. The Indians while fighting remained mounted, the cavalry dismounted. The horses were held behind and inside the (semi) circle of skirmishers. The odds were against the soldiers for they were greatly outnumbered, and they fought at a great disadvantage. Their ammunition was limited. Each man was supposed to carry one hundred rounds of cartridges, but a great many had wasted theirs by firing at game along the route. It does not take very long to expend that amount of ammunition especially when fighting against great odds.***

Thompson's last thoughts in his 1913 *Belle Foruche Bee* interview of the fight at the ford were,

"Cavalry men were also falling and the ranks gradually melting away. . . . Being in our present predicament, we were utterly powerless to help as we wished we could. We knew our duty, but to do it was beyond our power. Look where we could, we saw Indians; we two on foot could not cope with scores of them on horseback."

On the high bluff above the ford, the three Crow scouts watched as the troopers formed a skirmish line. They were on a small overlook just beyond view of the action that felled Custer. The Crow scout, Goes Ahead, later recalled in an interview to Irin Grant Libby,

"They (the three Crow scouts) dismounted and fired across into the Dakota (Sioux) camp, the circle of tents they could see over the tree-tops below them. They heard two volleys fired and saw the soldiers' horses standing back of the line in groups."

At 3:35 p.m. the chaos and confusion of war had started in earnest for the 7th Cavalry. With General George Armstrong Custer now shot in the left breast below his heart. He was alive but critically wounded. Command of the attack quickly shifted to Captain George Yates of Company F. Yates was facing a command issue with his second company, Company

E. Lieutenant Algernon Smith had been severely wounded. Yates quickly ordered Company F, now commanded by Second Lieutenant William Van Wyck Reily to file right to the north end of the ford. Here they were to form a skirmish line. Captain Yates had Second Lieutenant James Sturgis, now commander of Company E with Lieutenant Smith wounded, wheel left and form the center of the skirmish line. Captain Tom Custer with the trailing Company C followed Company E. Captain Custer went forward to Captain Yates. Second Lieutenant Henry Harrington wheeled Company C to the extreme left of the line at the south end of the ford.

The three companies with Captain Yates numbered 120 or so troopers. The number fours stood behind the skirmish line each holding the reins of four horses. Thirty men of Yates' battalion would have been in such positions. The Crow scouts, Hairy Moccasin, White Man Runs Him, and Goes Ahead, remembered this sight as they left the bluff overlooking the Ford B crossing. This would have left ninety troopers to be on the skimish line to fire their Springfield single-shot carbines. The troopers were young and had not trained on shooting from their saddles. The troopers of the 7th Cavalry would fire from a dismounted, standing skirmish line formation. Captain Yates ordered volley fire from the ninety troopers. They fired twice.

Upstream about a mile and a half from this fight in the timber by the river, Lieutenant DeRudio, Lieutenant Hare, Sergeant Culbertson, scouts Herenden and Girard, and others of the abandoned Reno position were hidden in the brush. They all heard these two volleys. They so stated at the Reno Court of Inquiry.

About a thousand yards to the rear of Yates and his men Captain Keogh had his men dismount and form a skirmish line. He had about eighty troopers between his Company I and Lieutenant Calhoun's Company L. Again, the fours would take the reins of four horses, about twenty such groups of horses. Sixty troopers would be on the firing line. They would fire volleys, up to a half dozen or so, from the high ground of Nye-Cartwright Ridge. These volleys were heard by the men of Reno's battalion which had recently arrived on the high ground of Reno-Benteen Hill. Captain Benteen's men were just arriving and heard these volleys. And as Captain McDougall and the pack-train were crossing the open ground to the southeast of Reno-Benteen Hill, they too heard the volleys on their "right" as they moved. Again this would be remembered at the RCOI in 1879.

The significance of the volleys was confused during later years. The Yates' volleys were heard by the Reno men upstream in the timber near the river. The Keogh volleys, being on the high ground of Nye-Cartwright Ridge, were easier to hear for the Reno-Benteen-McDougall men. They were on about the same level of high ground about two miles distant.

As Captain Custer saw his brother being pulled from the waters of the Little Bighorn, he quickly dashed to his brother's side to give aid. Lieutenant William Cooke, Captain Custer, and the small group in the river retreated behind the skirmish line. Doctor Lord was summoned to give aid to the general and to Lieutenant Smith. The doctor quickly realized that the general's chest wound, most probably a sucking chest wound with a punctured left lung, was far beyond his field abilities to treat. He could not save the general by himself.

Doctor Lord probably told Yates, Tom Custer and Cooke, that only the medical ambulance with its surgeon, First Lieutenant Holmes Offley Paulding with General Terry's column, could treat and possibly save the critically wounded General Custer. Lieutenant Smith probably suffered a severe shoulder wound from Bobtail Horse's shot. He too would need the surgeon's help in the ambulance wagon.

The three Crow scouts on the bluff had seen enough of the battle at the ford. The Sioux were winning and hundreds of warriors were beginning to comb through the land about the ford. The three Crow quickly mounted and galloped south along the high bluffs. They knew this was the safest way to escape the growing numbers of warriors below. The time was about 3:40 p.m.

As the troopers formed their skirmish line, two loud volleys were fired. The two volleys were heard by Privates Thompson and Watson in the brush. They were heard by the Crows on the bluffs. A mile and a half to the the south, DeRudio's soldiers in the timber heard the same volleys.

With Long Hair Custer, Son of the Morning Star, no longer chief of these soldiers, bad things could only happen from now on. White Cow Bull and the warriors defending the village began to fire, not at the skirmish line, but at the line of horse holders behind. The loud noise of battle had made the horses skittish. Then a horse holder on the right, from Company C had his horses take off. Four troopers of Company C were no longer cavalrymen, but now foot soldiers. Bobtail Horse or one of the others managed to scare off the horses of a horse holder of Company E, the gray horse company. Four more troopers were now foot soldiers. White Cow Bull reloaded and then took aim and one more horse holder of Company C let his mounts go.

Captain Keogh a thousand yards to the east on Nye-Cartwright Ridge knew that this was not the battle plan as General Custer had described to him. Custer was to ride directly into the center of the village to fight. Keogh had seen some lead riders fall from their saddles into the river. One of them looked to be the general, himself. Yates and his column had stopped and formed a skirmish line, not a part of the attack plan.

Captain Yates now acting as commander on this section of the battlefield by the river, was confronted with a huge problem. The Indians were gaining the battle initiative in ever growing numbers. General Custer needed the medical ambulance far to the north with General Terry. Yates knew Company E was in trouble with Lieutenant Smith wounded. Captain Custer was screaming for Yates to get the wounded General Custer to proper medical help. More and more the Indians were putting pressure on the south end of the skirmish line. These Indians had recently left the fight with Reno's troops. Yates looked about him and noted that his column, if mounted, would be facing north, not south. The nearest high ground, that of the high hill later to be known as Calhoun Hill, lay to the north and east. Directly behind him to the east about a thousand yards distant was Captain Keogh and his two companies. The heights of Nye-Cartwright would have been potentially a better defensive position as Keogh already was there. Heading back up the Medicine Tail Coulee would have been a good choice as Benteen and McDougall and the pack-train with vitally needed ammunition were in that direction. But, both of these latter choices would most probably ensure the death of General George Custer per Dr. Lord's pronouncement.

Captain George Yates made up his mind. He ordered his battalion to mount up and follow him up the high ground to the north and east. In hind sight, safety probably could have been found riding to the south and east to rendezvous with either Keogh or the expected column of Benteen. But Yates went north. Saving the general, seemed paramount.

As the mounted troopers began their ride to Calhoun Hill, twelve, maybe sixteen lowly, vastly outnumbered troopers, eight or twelve from Company C and four from Company E tried desperately to follow the mounted column. As the mounted troopers disappeared over the first low ridge, First Sergeant Edwin Bobo of Company C, still on horseback, ordered the stranded troopers on foot to fire then head for the nearest high ground. This was the nearer Greasy Grass Ridge immediately to their right. Sergeant Bobo was an experienced NCO and knew that their only chance was to fight together and withdraw to higher ground. Most of the pursuing Indians seemed more interested in the retreating column of mounted troopers. Lieutenant Harrington, now commanding Company C, looked over his shoulder as they rode out. He could not help but notice the desperate plight of First Sergenat Bobo and the men with him.

Chief Gall crossed the river with his warriors. He had a growing vengeance in his heart and wanted to kill as many of these soldiers as he could. He directed his warriors to follow the Deep Coulee below Calhoun Hill in pursuit.

As Captain Yates led his retreating troops up to Calhoun Hill, he waved his hat furiously at Captain Keogh. He needed Keogh to rendezvous with his column on the high ground of Calhoun Hill. Captain Keogh saw the growing menace of the Indians and mounted his battalion. Keogh and his men charged north, down the south wall of Deep Coulee and then up the north wall. He arrived on Calhoun Hill with his men about the time Yates arrived with his men. As the two columns met on Calhoun Hill, another important transition took place. Captain Keogh was now senior officer to all five companies in this portion of the battlefield. It would now be his decisions as to what to do next.

Captain Yates had made the first fateful turn for the troopers of the 7th Cavalry. By turning north, he moved away from the potential reinforcement from the Benteen column. Captain Keogh by abandoning his high ground on Nye-Cartwright Ridge, opened a huge gap between the five companies on the north and the rest of the regiment to the south. This gap was rapidly being filled with hundreds of hostile Indians, especially those led by Gall.

It was a fateful turn. But at this point in time, about 3:45 p.m., it was not a completely deadly decision for these men. More decisions and orders were to be made that would seal their fate.

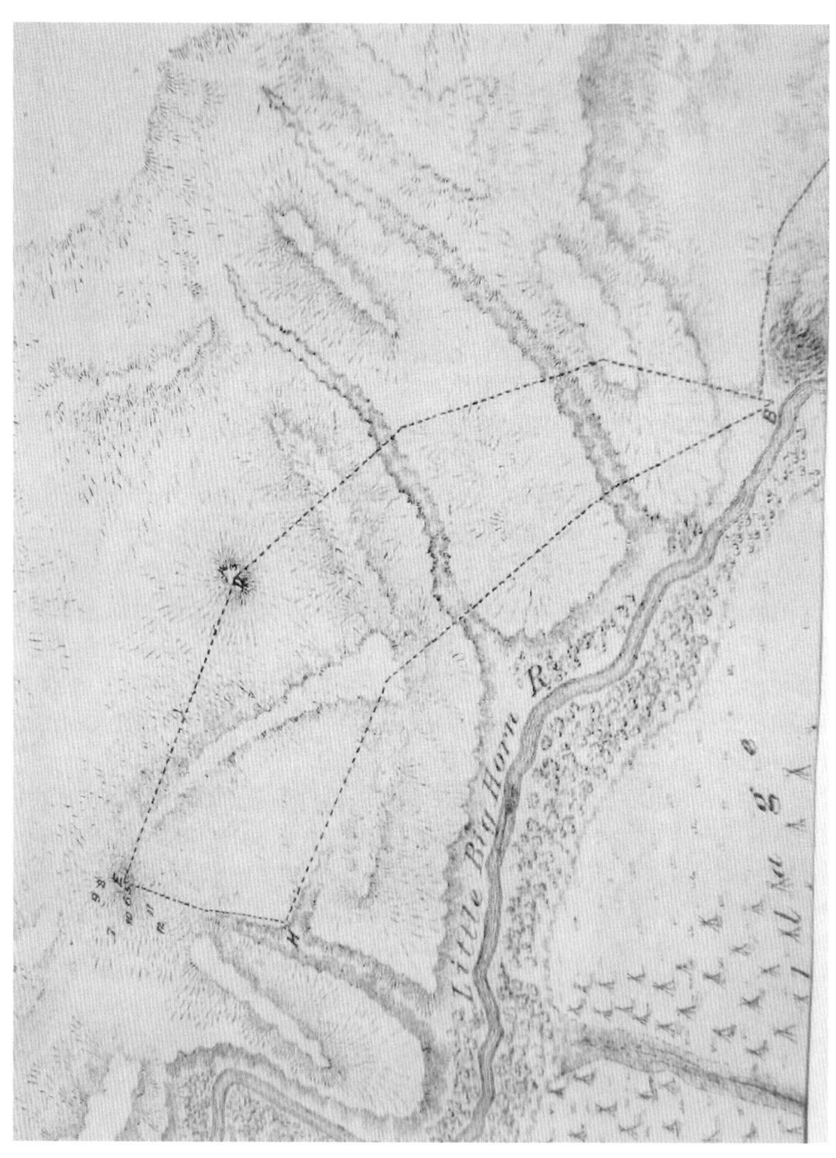
Little Big Horn River

7

The Northern Battles of the Little Bighorn

It was about 3:45 p.m. on the southern end of the Little Bighorn battle. Reno's men were beginning to collect themselves on the high ground to be known as the Reno-Benteen Hill. The three Crow scouts who had minutes before left the Ford B battle, were riding past the Reno troops. They feared being mistaken as Sioux by the troopers. They headed south to escape as far as they could from their tribal enemies. As the Crows approached the last high ground before Reno Creek below, they halted.

Captain Benteen turned from Ford A. As Benteen met up with Captain Weir and the column on the Reno Creek, they both saw three Indians on the high ground. The troopers on Reno Creek prepared for action. As Captain Benteen rode forward, he saw the three Indians were those Crow who had ridden with Custer. Benteen, not fluent in Indian languages, tried to find out where Custer was. The Crows pointed the way. They stated much "pooh-poohing" was going on further north. At the Reno Court of Inquiry, Benteen would testify he thought Custer was in the village fighting the "skedaddling" Indians, who in fact were not "skedaddling." Most importantly, what was not communicated was that Custer was shot. Custer was no longer in command of the northern columns. Indeed Custer was no longer in command of the whole regiment. Major Reno was now in command, but no one knew this. No one knew this except for Captain Keogh, Captain Yates and Lieutenant Cooke three miles away.

As Benteen and his column rode up the bluff, they saw the assembling men of Reno's column. Major Reno yelled for Benteen to halt his column and assist his men. The time was about 3:50 p.m. Benteen, seeing the confusion about the hill, had his column dismount and prepare to defend. Benteen knew it would be some time before Captain McDougall and the pack-train arrived. Benteen did not want to rush forward with his men seeing the condition of Major Reno and his command. The urgency of "Come quick. Bring packs" was now quietly forgotten in Benteen's blouse pocket.

Captain Weir, however, had seen the message. In the distance he heard volley firing. He knew his fellow troops were in that direction to the north. Captain Weir had an uneasy feeling about Benteen's order to halt and dismount. The feeling would gnaw at Captain Weir as the men deployed.

Three miles to the north, Captain Keogh had his own serious problems with which to deal. General Custer was critically wounded. Dr. Lord said he needed the medical assistance of First Lieutenant Paulding found only in the ambulance with General Terry. They were north somewhere along the Bighorn River. General Terry was probably a day's march from Calhoun Hill per Lieutenant Cooke's recollections. As adjutant for Custer, Cooke knew General Terry and Custer were to meet and engage together on June 26. The location was to be somewhere along the Little Bighorn. Captain Yates informed Keogh that with Lieutenant Smith being seriously wounded and needing medical attention, Yates' battalion was now being commanded by inexperienced young lieutenants. Captain Custer had been insistent on tending to his brother, the general. Younger brother, Boston Custer, and nephew Armstrong "Autie" Reed now too were seeing the panic about the general.

Down towards the river, Keogh could see the stranded troopers fighting a desperate retreat on foot. Sergeant Edwin Bobo was fighting for his life and the others with him. Lieutenant Harrington was pleading for Keogh to save them.

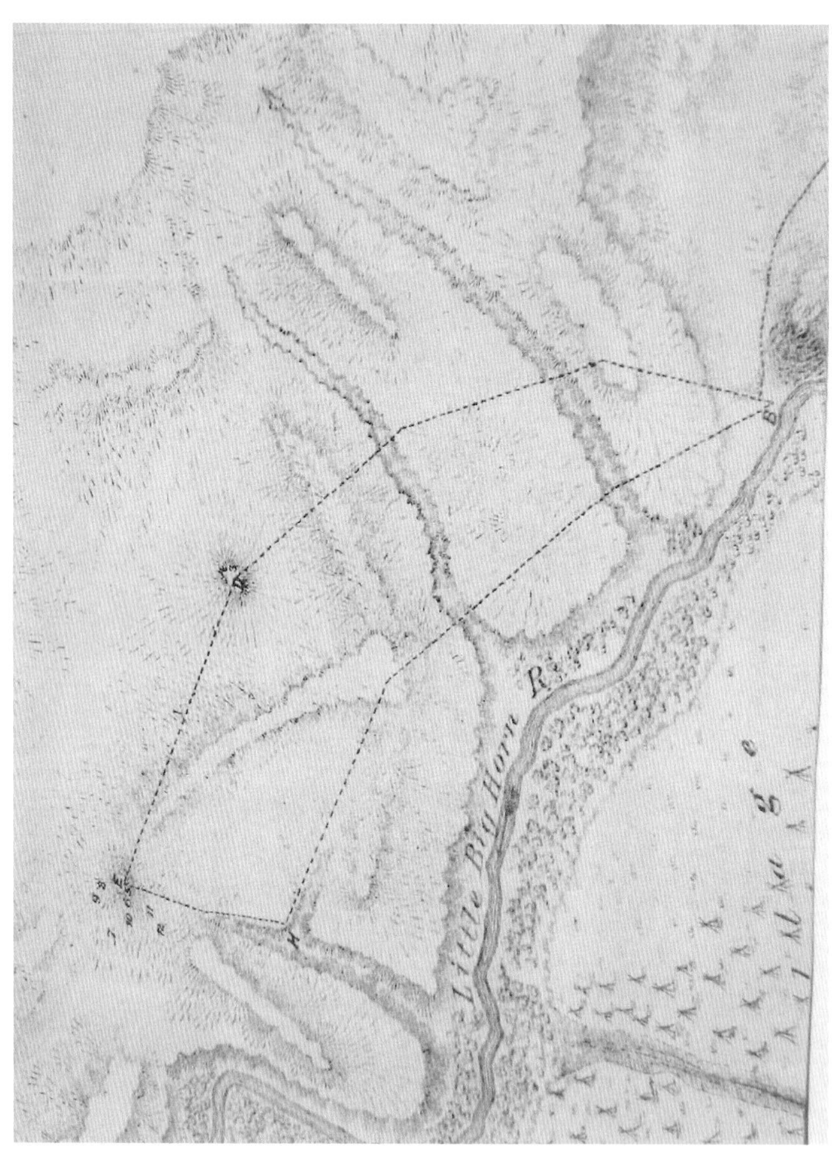
Little Big Horn River

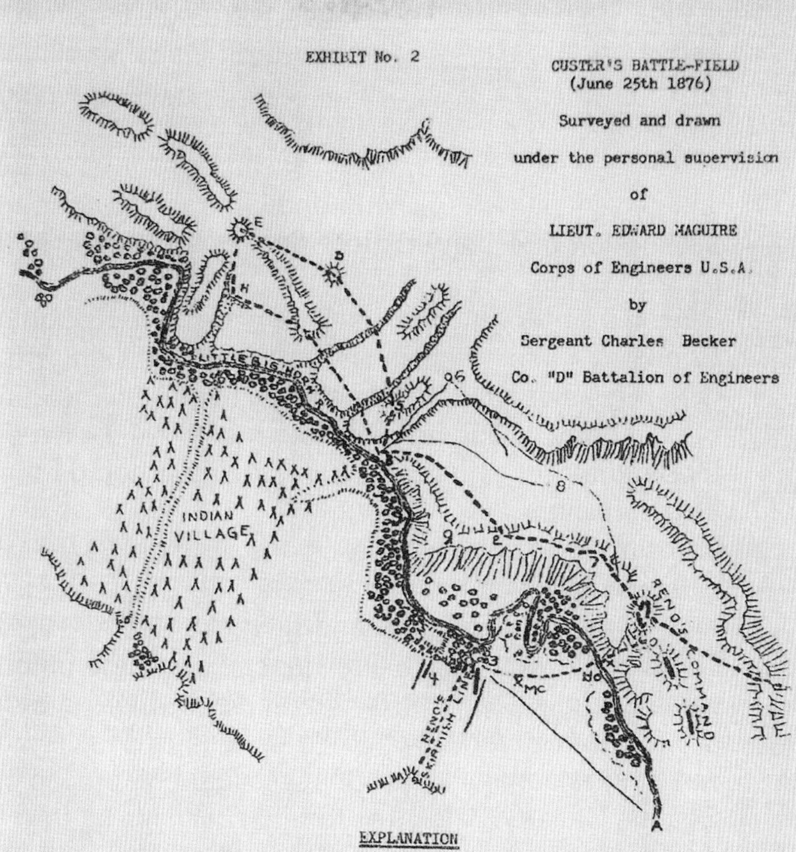

EXPLANATION

A. Reno's crossing and advance down valley.
B. The ford Custer was believed to have tried.
D. Calhoun's stand.
E. Custer Hill, scene of the last stand.
H. Many bodies found here.
Mc. Lt. McIntosh killed here. Marked with X.
Ho. Lt. Hodgson killed here. Marked with X.
1. Girard marks point where he encouraged Reynolds, the Scout.
2. Girard estimates Custer's position when Reno reached hill in retreat.
3. Girard marks point where Reynolds was killed.
4. Herendeen marks point where he dismounted.
5. Hare's estimate of Reno's position, in his advance toward Custer.
6. Hare's estimate of Weir's advance point.
7. DeRudio's estimate of where he saw Custer, during the valley fight.
8. Martin marks point from which he was sent back with message to Benteen to "Come on and be quick".
9. Edgerly's estimate of point of Reno's advance.

Note: The four lines to front and rear of the dotted line on the original map marked "Reno's Skirmish Line", were marked in pencil by witnesses who thought the map incorrectly placed the skirmish line.

-558-

Gall and his warriors were fast filling the length of Deep Coulee below Calhoun Hill. The Indians were now beginning to fire heavily at the gathered troopers on Calhoun Hill. It was approximately 3:55 p.m. Captain Keogh made the next crucial decisions:

1 – Lieutenant James Calhoun and Company L formed a skirmish line immediately on this hill facing the Indians below.

2 – First Lieutenant James E. Porter put Keogh's Company I into skirmish line to the left of Calhoun's men. This extended the line slightly to the left and rear of Company L. The horse holders took the horses of these companies into the swale located behind the skirmish line.

3 - Captain Yates took his battalion, the wounded General Custer and Lieutenant Smith, and the Custer family and went north to find General Terry. Captain Tom Custer rode with this column, placed in charge of the Custer family. General Terry was somewhere along the Bighorn River. Captain Yates was to seek from Terry the release of Major Brisbin's four companies of Second Cavalry. Yates was to return with his battalion and that of Major Brisbin's. Scout Mitch Bouyer was to guide Yates to Terry. It was hoped that Terry was perhaps a hard two-to-three hour ride north, maybe twenty miles downstream from here. In reality, Terry's column had found the going rough and were about twenty-five to thirty miles north around this time.

4 - Lieutenant Harrington was to command Company C. This company was returned to Keogh's battalion. Harrington was ordered to head down the hill toward the river to support the troopers on foot there.

5 – After Lieutenant Porter established the Company I skirmish line, Keogh then ordered him to carry a message back to Captain Benteen and Major Reno.

He was to apprise them of the situation in the north. Keogh would wait for further instruction.

With these decisions made, Captain Myles Keogh, an experienced combat officer, now hoped to hold his ground. He and Lieutenant Cooke knew that Custer had sent two messages back to Benteen to urge him north. Custer had felt that Benteen would be near at the opening of the Custer attack. Perhaps Benteen and his men were over the visible high ground of Weir Point. This meant that Benteen was within five minutes of helping Keogh and his men. Keogh felt he could easily hold Calhoun Hill five, maybe ten minutes until Benteen arrived. With Benteen's men, the combined columns and the expected arrival of Captain McDougall's Company B and the eighty-four troopers assigned to pack duty would create a large defensive force. With the extra ammunition, Keogh and Benteen could hold out until Yates returned with Major Brisbin.

The offensive initiative for the 7th Cavalry was gone, but Keogh had momentary defensive initiative with him. Things looked manageable at 4:00 p.m. That was about to change rapidly over the next fifteen minutes.

Captain Yates pulled out to the north along what is now called Battle Ridge and the Last Stand Hill with his Company F and Company E following. Keogh summoned Lieutenant James Porter and gave him a very important message to be delivered to Major Reno. Keogh told the young lieutenant to go back the route they had travelled and then go to the high ground beyond Weir Point. Captain Benteen should be there. Porter must at all costs get Benteen to ride forward at a gallop. Porter then needed to find Major Reno and inform him that with the general critically wounded, Major Reno was now commander of the entire regiment. Lieutenant Porter saluted Keogh and mounted his horse. He took off down the steep ravine slope of Deep Coulee.

Suddenly a shot rang out from the Deep Coulee below. Lieutenant James Porter was hit hard in the right shoulder as his bloodied jacket would show when found in the Indian camp three days later. Porter fell from his mount. A handful of Indians were directed by Gall or someone close to him to take the young soldier chief with the single silver bar on his shoulders as prisoner back to the village. Captain Keogh looked on and felt a pang of fear and frustration in the young lieutenant's disappearance. Keogh needed a message to get through urgently, but he could see the ground below this hill was filled with hostiles. He summoned Lieutenant James Calhoun over and asked for the best trooper-horseman in Company L. He needed to deliver the same message.

Lieutenant Calhoun sent for First Sergeant James Butler. Captain Keogh gave Butler the same urgent message. But, this time he told Butler to ride down the slope toward the river with the men of Company C, led by Lieutenant Henry Harrington. Lieutenant Harrington was to establish a line on Greasy Grass Ridge.The Indians seemed less numerous right along the river. Perhaps getting to the high ground of Weir Point by going close to the river would be more successful. Keogh then ordered Lieutenant Henry Harrington and Company C to charge down the slope. They were to provide cover fire for Sergeant Butler. Company C hurriedly went down from Calhoun Hill toward the men on foot with First Sergeant Bobo. Butler rode too with his now desperate message for help.

Keogh then turned and watched as Yates began to descend the slopes to the north of Last Stand Hill. Keogh could have taken Companies I and L and mounted a hasty retreat to the east and safety. However, such a command meant death to the twelve to sixteen men on foot of Companies C and E below the ridge.

At that moment other interested parties watched as Captain Yates left the high ground of Calhoun Hill. In the Indian village the war chiefs Crazy Horse and Two Moons were getting prepared for battle. Crazy Horse had emerged from his circle putting on his war medicine and paints. He had painted his horse too with war paints. The village was filled with excitement and commotion since the Ford B attack.

Up on the hill soldiers could been seen getting ready to ride north. Other soldiers were dismounting to fight on Calhoun Hill. Crazy Horse and his preferred attack plan always favored separating a smaller portion of troops from the main body. He had done this a week earlier on the Rosebud. He and his warriors nearly succeeded in wiping out one group of Crook's soldiers. These soldiers were saved only when rescued by another body of troops who were late into the battle.

Years before, in 1866, Crazy Horse had been the bait to lure out Captain William Fetterman and his company. Fetterman and his troopers rode out of Fort Phil Kearny in Wyoming Territory. Captain Fetterman and his eighty troopers were lured over a ridge away from the protection of the other troops in the fort. As they crossed a ridge, they were wiped out by Chief Red Cloud and the hundreds of warriors waiting for the unwitting soldiers. These warriors had been lying in wait for Fettermen and his men as they chased after Crazy Horse.

Crazy Horse gave out a war cry. He pointed out the troopers to his Oglala warriors and the Cheyenne warriors of Two Moons who were about to follow him. They rode north through the village at a gallop. When they came to the flats to the north of the village, where present-day Highway 212 crosses the Little Bighorn, they saw the column of Yates. Crazy Horse gave out a cry and the large force of hundreds of warriors crossed the river. This placed them to the front of the now approaching Captain Yates and scout Mitch Bouyer. A few shots were fired and newpaperman Frank Kellogg fell from his mount, a mule. Yates, knowing with the encumbrance of his wounded general and Lieutenant Smith and the civilians, his column could not outrun this large body of Indians. Yates quickly turned the column toward the high hill to his right and rear. The hill was to be known forever as Last Stand Hill. Yates had made his second fateful decision.

Yates chose to dismount and fight on the hill. He could have continued a hasty retreat to the east, but it most likely would have cost the general his life. So Yates gave the command to halt and prepare skirmish lines for a fight.

The party of warriors with Crazy Horse and Two Moons split into two groups. One followed the Yates column up away from the river. Crazy Horse continued east on the flats until he came to the end of the sloping ridge that went up to Last Stand Hill. In the ravine to the east of this ridge, Crazy Horse hoped to trap the soldiers. He hoped to hit them from the east side of the hill. Had Crazy Horse turned his warriors at the spot where Yates had halted, Company F and all on Last Stand Hill would have been the first to be wiped out. As it was, Company F would be one of the last companies to be wiped out.

It was now about 4:10 p.m. Captain Keogh was surveying the ongoing fight. He hopefully scanned the high bluffs around Weir Point looking for Captain Benteen. Keogh began to worry that Benteen had been distracted somehow. Or worse yet, due to the well known dislike Benteen had for General Custer since the Washita, perhaps Benteen was purposely slowing his advance to stay out of Custer's fight.

At that moment, Keogh heard shots and Indian war cries were heard to his left. Large groups of the horses from Company I and Company L were rushing riderless from the swale. Gall and his band had managed to sneak around the far left of Company I's skirmish line. With blankets and war cries they had spooked the horses from their holders' grips. Many of the men in Company I and Company L now shared the same predicament that Sergeant Bobo and the stranded horseless troopers had faced since the battle at Ford B. Benteen was going to be needed now more than ever.

As Crazy Horse and Two Moons and the large band of warriors rounded the slope and went into the ravine (today called Crazy Horse Ravine), Crazy Horse could see many dark soldier uniforms at the top of this ravine. The time was about 4:15 p.m. The soldiers had their backs to Crazy Horse and seemed to be busy firing at the Indians on the other side of the hill they occupied. Crazy Horse changed his mind and stopped pursuing the Yates column and instead focused on the exposed backside of Keogh's Company I.

Crazy Horse Ravine is about a mile and a quarter in length. As Crazy Horse began to ascend it, Captain Keogh was still on his mount, Commanche. Keogh turned in horror to see the surge of onrushing warriors in his rear. There was no choice. He shouted out to First Sergeant Varden and Sergeant Bustard, to move and refuse the skirmish line to the left. They had to do it immediately. The distance to travel on foot to secure the hill ridge of Battle Ridge from the left side of Calhoun Hill was about a quarter mile, a thousand feet. The sergeants told the men to run like hell.

As the men turned and began their move, Crazy Horse accelerated the charge. The soldiers were running raggedly and the line was now irregular as would be stated at the Reno Court of Inquiry by Lieutenant Wallace. Captain Keogh and the sergeants told the men to stop some 130 yards short of the crest of the ridge. There was no time now. The command "Fire!" was given. Some of the war party with Crazy Horse went down. However, the well known war medicine that followed Crazy Horse left him untouched. Forty men were soon consumed by a mounted horde of ferocious and fearless warriors.

Captain Keogh was shot in the leg while on Commanche. He fell to the ground. Sergeants Varden and Bustard took up positions on either side of their downed captain. They watched as the forty men of Company I perished in the following few minutes. Soon too the bullets of the Indians felled Varden and Bustard. They fell dead next to their dying captain.

Lieutenant Calhoun behind his first platoon of Company L turned and saw the danger. He yelled to Second Lieutenant John Crittenden standing behind the second platoon. Together they wheeled about and emptied their revolvers into the attacking horde in their rear. The men in the skirmish line were scared and confused. There were hundreds of Indians immediately in their front and now in their rear. Company L soon perished as well, most in the skirmish line position they had held. This was the only recognizable skirmish line of resistance which General Terry and the surviving troopers found after the battle.

The time was now between 4:20 p.m. and 4:25 p.m. Captain Yates had deployed the first platoon of Company E down the slope from his position. They were facing north and holding back the large group of Indians there. Yates deployed one Company F platoon, under Second Lieutenant William Van Wyck Reily, to the right of Company E's line. They likewise were facing north. Seeing the carnage going on with Company I and Company L, Yates directed his second platoon to face south. They would meet the expected assault to come from Calhoun Hill. Company E's second platoon was held in temporary reserve with Second Lieutenant James Sturgis commanding it. The wounded General Custer, Lieutenant Smith, the civilians, and Dr. Lord were grouped in the center.

A large number of Indians on the southern portion of the battlefield emerged over the rise of Calhoun Hill. Many were stunned at what they saw next. Many would recount the image to David Humphreys Miller years later.

The men of Company C were appalled at the rapid annihilation of two cavalry companies, companies with men who were well known to the men of Company C. Per the interviews held with David Humphreys Miller years later, a number of Indians told the same story:

"Suddenly the soldiers went crazy. Instead of firing at the attacking Indians, they began shooting at one another, and at themselves. Before any warrior could charge them, all but four were dead."

These four soldiers remounted and tried to escape. Three were pulled from their horses and killed. One managed to ride away. The fourth was chased for some distance back up the Medicine Tail Coulee by Cheyenne warriors Old Bear and Kills- At- Night and a Sioux warrior. This one rider, eventually unable to outrun his pursuers, drew his revolver and put one shot to his head. He fell from his horse onto the prairie grass far from the battlefields.

This rider was Lieutenant Harrington. He and sergeants Bobo and Butler, and one other trooper, Corporal Foley of Company C., could not stomach dying with the others. Most likely an old NCO, one who well knew of the Fetterman massacre ten years prior, reacted and gave out the order for the troopers to end it. Years before, Captain Fettermen and his friend Captain Brown in their last moments had put their revolvers to each other's heads to avoid torture. Someone in Company C told the young troopers to end it now. Per Sergeant Kanipe who was of Company C, when he identifed his company's remains three days later, he recalled seeing Sergeant Finley. Finley was the oldest line sergeant in the company. Perhaps it was Sergeant Finley who saw the massacre in progress and told his young troopers to end it or risk being taken alive.

Per Kanipe, "I recognized Sergeants Finkle and Finley. Sergeant Finley lay at his horse's (Carlo) head." Most likely an old timer such as Finley told the young troopers, most of whom were in their late teens, or early twenties, to shoot their horses first and then themselves. Do this to avoid torture at the hands of the Indians. Lieutenant Harrington had lost control of his command, Company C. So too had First Sergeant Bobo. Bobo was found among the dead near Company I when their bodies were found. Most likely Bobo mounted his horse and charged up and over Calhoun Hill. As he crossed over the ridge he rode into the carnage of Company I's slaughter. He was felled in the group surrounding Captain Keogh. Sergeant Kanipe later identified Bobo's body amongst the dead of Company I. Bobo's horse was found dead fifty yards further east on a nearby ridge. This was the ridge Keogh's men had rapidly left as Crazy Horse's warriors attacked.

Sergeant Butler of Company L thought of his order from Keogh. Perhaps Benteen could be reached if he could cross the ford from where the Yates battalion had recently attacked. Butler made it across Deep Coulee to the slopes of the Medicine Tail Coulee when he was shot. His body was found some five hundred yards from the Ford B battle site. Corporal Foley's body was found two hundred yards away from Sergeant Butler, closer to the river. The time was approximately 4:30 p.m.

The mass suicide of troops was watched by Cheyenne and Sioux warriors alike. Black Wolf remembered it. So too did Pine, Limpy, Bobtail Horse, Rising Sun, Red Fox, Dives Backwards and many others. Even Crazy Horse must have been momentarily stunned by the rapidity with which so many soldiers had been killed in these last five or ten minutes. But as he looked north along Battle Ridge there were still soldiers to be killed. He watched as the growing numbers of warriors stormed onward toward the diminishing number of soldiers.

On Last Stand Hill Captain Yates, Captain Tom Custer, and Lieutenant Cooke stood in shock. They had watched three companies get wiped out in a little over ten minutes. Their good friend and comrade Captain Keogh was gone. Company I was gone. Lieutenant Calhoun, who was Tom Custer's brother-in-law, was gone. Company L was gone. And worst of all, many of Company C had killed themselves.

Yates had to act quickly. Horses were shot and used for barricades. Lieutenant Sturgis was to take his reserve platoon and rush to the Deep Ravine below Last Stand Hill. This was to keep the Indians coming from the killing ground of Company C and overruning the Company E first platoon from the rear. Second Lieutenant James Sturgis and his twenty men charged down the slope to gain the ravine. Sturgis was an infantryman from the 20th Infantry on temporary assignment with the 7th Cavalry. Sturgis was son to old Colonel Sturgis, the Commander of the 7th Cavalry back at headquarters in the Dakota Territory. Many Indians recalled watching this strange charge by a group of dismounted soldiers.

As this body of men made their rapid advance on foot down the slope, the Cheyenne and Oglala warriors in front of Company E's first platoon broke through near the juncture with Company F. Eight men from this line ran backwards to join Lieutenant Sturgis and his men in the Deep Ravine. The time was about 4:35 p.m.

The Indians could now see that the small hill in their front was an easy target. Slowly from all sides the warriors advanced. Captain Yates needed all guns now, so even the very wounded were propped up to shoot. All that is except for General Custer. He had lost so much blood that he was mostly unconscious at that point. He may have been able to watch the shooting, but it did not matter any more.

Lieutenant Algernon Smith, though wounded in his shoulder, could still hold a gun. He stood by young Lieutenant Reily. Captain Custer, Lieutenant Cooke, and Captain Yates stood together. One by one the troopers went silent. One by one they fell dead on that hill. Hundreds of warriors were sneaking through the grass toward the top. Captain Custer yelled out to his baby brother, Boston, and his young nephew Harry Armstrong "Autie" Reed to make a run for it. As the two ran to the north and down the slope, they were both quickly killed. Lieutenant Smith seeing the hopelessness of the hill position told young Lieutenant Reily to follow him down the slope in their front. It looked momentarily empty of warriors. Over a slight rise Smith saw about one hundred or more armed Indians waiting for him. Smith with his wound could not make much of a fight.

Big Beaver was on that side of the hill and he recalled,

"A swell of excitement surged through the onlookers when on the north slope of the battle ridge a tall soldier jumped to his feet and ran across a little gulch toward the high knob to the north (current site of the Indian Memorial). Perhaps he thought some of his comrades might be alive there, still holding out, or that gulch beyond the knob might provide him with an avenue of escape. He stopped short when he saw hundreds of warriors still in the gulch. Standing there on the hillside, he put his revolver to his head and pulled the trigger."

The warriors on that side of the hill advanced forward. Some remembered a young trooper lying in the grass as he cried. The Indians stood over him, watched, then shot him in the face. Lieutenant William Van Wyck Reily found his end there in the grass.

As the plight on the hill was now down to a few remaining troops and the three officers Yates, Tom Custer,and Cooke, a final stand was made. Tom Custer, already having watched the death of his good friend Myles Keogh, his baby sister's husband, James Calhoun, his entire Company C, his younger brother, Boston, and his nephew by an older stepsister, young Autie Reed, had to perform the most dreaded act of his life. The two-time Civil War Medal of Honor winner and long-time member of his beloved George Armstrong Custer's cavalry put an end to his brother George, whom Tom affectionately called Autie during their youth. The tears flowed from Tom Custer's eyes as he knelt down whispered his last goodbye to George, to Autie. He put his revolver to the left temple of his brother's head and pulled the trigger.

As Tom stood again, Lieutenant Cooke fired at the Indians now steps from them. As Cooke's revolver clicked on an empty chamber he threw his spent weapon at the two nearest Indians. They quickly killed him as he tried to offer a final fight. As Tom Custer watched this fight, he fired at Indians to his front. Then he heard the dull thwack of a bullet hitting bone and the last grunt of Captain George Yates as he fell to the right of Captain Custer.

Now filled with sorrow and immense rage, Tom Custer, the last to stand, wearing his full buckskin uniform, would take on the entire Indian mass himself. Many of the Indians who made that final assault on the hill recalled the last man standing as one in buckskins. Most Custer admirers wanted to say it was the general himself. Indeed the Boy General, with Custer Luck, George Armstrong Custer must have been, should have been, the last in the eyes of the many Custer admirers. It was Custer's Last Stand after all. Instead it was Tom Custer's Last Stand.

In the end, George Armstrong Custer had been critically wounded in the left chest by White Cow Bull. The general was finished off by his brother Tom Custer as the command was about to be overrun. George Armstrong Custer's wounds would be recounted by Captain Benteen and others at the Reno Court of Inquiry. General Custer was never in charge on Last Stand Hill. Custer went first, down by the river's edge.

The time was about 4:40 p.m. Lieutenant Sturgis and the twenty-eight troopers with him, desperately made for the cover of the timber at the end of the Deep Ravine. They were trying to make the cover by the river. As Sturgis led them in that direction, all at once many Indians showed up on the high ground about the ravine. Sturgis was shot in the back. He fell to the ground and disappeared into the grass. The other twenty-eight men turned quickly the other way looking for cover. More and more Indians from all the camps began to line the edge of the ravine. There was no where to turn now. The Indians began firing into the blue mass of crying men below.

The men yelled. The men screamed. The men tried clawing their way up the steep ravine sides. All the while the hail of bullets and arrows from the Indians continued. Eventually all movement from the blue mass ceased. No more cries were heard. The Indians stood and gave out a great victory cry. All the soldiers were dead. It was 4:45 p.m.

The mop-up of finding the wounded in the grasslands began for the Indians. They would escort their wounded comrades back to the village and their families. The Indians began to look for battle treasures to mark their great victory. They killed any wounded soldiers still lying in the grass.

Down by the river at the end of the Deep Ravine, one soldier, wounded badly, was crawling through the grass. Per David Humphreys Miller, the Indian woman, Woman- Who- Walks- With- The- Stars, said she was looking for stray cavalry horses and came upon a struggling, badly wounded soldier in a blue uniform. He still had his carbine. He would crawl, and then rest, as he struggled to make the water's edge. He made it to the water where he let go his carbine. Woman- Who- Walks- With- The-Stars picked up a heavy branch from the river bank. As the soldier lay in the water, she approached him. She felt a momentary sense of pity for this *washichu* soldier. Then she remembered how these soldiers had come to kill all in the village. With a sense of hatred at that moment, she clubbed the lone soldier about his head and shoulders. The soldier disappeared below the surface of the water.

This soldier most likely was Second Lieutenant James Sturgis. His body was never found after the battle. His bloodied undershirt was found in the camp along with Lieutenant Porter's bloodied jacket. The body of Lieutenant Sturgis was probably dragged from the river and pulled into the camp by the Indian women looking for soldier items to claim as their own.

The time now was after 5:00 p.m. Captain Weir could no longer stand the slow pace of the troops on Reno-Benteen Hill. The firing from the north was now down to "scattering shots." Captain Weir had his Company D mount up. He proceeded forward, per Lieutenant Cooke's instructions to Benteen, with or without Captain Benteen.

As his Company D rode north, the rest of the column slowly began to move. No one remembers giving the order to move, but move they did. Captain McDougall's pack-train had arrived a while back and the ammunition distributed to the men. Captain Moylan and his Company A at the rear struggled while tending to the wounded. As Weir made it to the high ground of Weir Point, he and his men could see a great dust cloud on the other side of Deep Coulee. Slowly, riders on horseback were going about and shooting at objects on the ground.

Captain Benteen pulled up next on Weir Point. He ordered companies to form a line to his right. This was to let Custer and his men know where Benteen and his men were. For five minutes the men of Weir's and Benteen's men looked north. They saw no soldiers.

Then out of the depths of Deep Coulee and Medicine Tail Coulee a vast mass of Indian warriors arose. They were at a gallop headed toward the men on Weir Point. Benteen quickly ordered the retreat back to Reno-Benteen Hill. The battles of the northern battlefield were over. Five companies of the 7th Cavalry lay dead.

The Indians had suffered some dead, but many were wounded. As the warriors took up positions around Reno and Benteen, news came into the camp from scouts to the north. More troops were seen coming their way from the Bighorn River. They had with them the dreaded big guns on wheels, Lieutenant Low's Gatling guns.

On the slope of the Last Stand Hill the Indians were scalping and taking their trophies of the day. Turkey Legs, a warrior who had been among those who had finished off the soldiers on the hill recalled to David Humphreys Miller in later years,

> ***Among the bravest of the soldiers was a big man . . . . He acted much as the leader of the soldiers . . . . The metal white bars he wore (those of a captain) seemed some sort of personal medicine. His body was among those there part way down the slope, near the barricade of horses. Amazingly he seemed to come to life right before their eyes. He propped himself up on one elbow and looked around him as though he had just arrived from another world. Looking about with a wild expression on his face, almost like that of a madman, he gripped a pistol in his right hand. A courageous Sioux warrior ran forward, grabbed the revolver out of the white man's grasp, then turned it on him and shot him through the head. The Cheyennes mustered up enough courage after that to strike and stab him until they were sure he was dead. He was the last man of Custer's command to be killed on the ridge. . . . Not far from this spot lay***

> ***the body of a soldier whose sweeping side whiskers (Lieutenant William Cooke) at once caught the attention of the sparce bearded Indians.***

Wooden Leg was nearby and scalped off one of those long, dark sideburns from the face of Cooke. White Cow Bull too was combing the field of the dead soldiers. He was looking for the soldier chief he had shot at the ford. As he approached the last hill of dead soldiers, he found the body. He took out his knife to cut the right trigger finger off at the joint. White Cow Bull felt that there must be strong medicine in that soldier chief finger that had fired that heavy rifle so quickly at the ford. But then a Cheyenne woman, Mahwissa, and then Monahseetah approached. Mahwissa signed to the Indian to stop and not mutilate this dead soldier. She said, "He is our kinsman!" As George Custer had written in his book, *My Life On The Plains*, after the Battle of the Washita in 1868, Mahwissa had wed in Cheyenne tradition Custer and the young Indian maiden, Monahseetah. Now here in this land so many miles away from the Oklahoma plains, and seven and a half years later, Mahwissa, Monahseetah, and Monahseetah's seven year-old son, Yellow Bird, stood.

Mahwissa, took her bone sewing awl and began to poke it far into the ears of the dead soldier chief. She said, "So Long Hair, the Creeping Panther, will hear better in the Spirit Land." For Custer had indeed violated the terms of the peace council he had held with the chiefs of the Southern Cheyenne after the Battle of the Washita. Long Hair Custer was not to fight anymore the Cheyenne, or else, he and all who rode with him would perish.

Monahseetah and her seven year-old son with the yellow streaks of hair, looked down at her dead soldier chief husband. Sadly, this was the one and only time young Yellow Bird would lay eyes on his birth father. At the same time, Monahseetah's remorse was filled with hatred at this man whom she had loved so. He had spurned her. He said he would have no other wife than his white wife, Elizabeth "Libbie" Custer. Now Monahseetah would remain alone with her son per Cheyenne custom.

Mahwissa knowing the sad story took a broken arrow and left one more reminder for the dead Long Hair Custer. She pushed it into the penis of the dead man, to remind him that he should have no more children in the Spirit Land. For he, Long Hair Custer, had never been a good father to his one and only son, Yellow Bird.

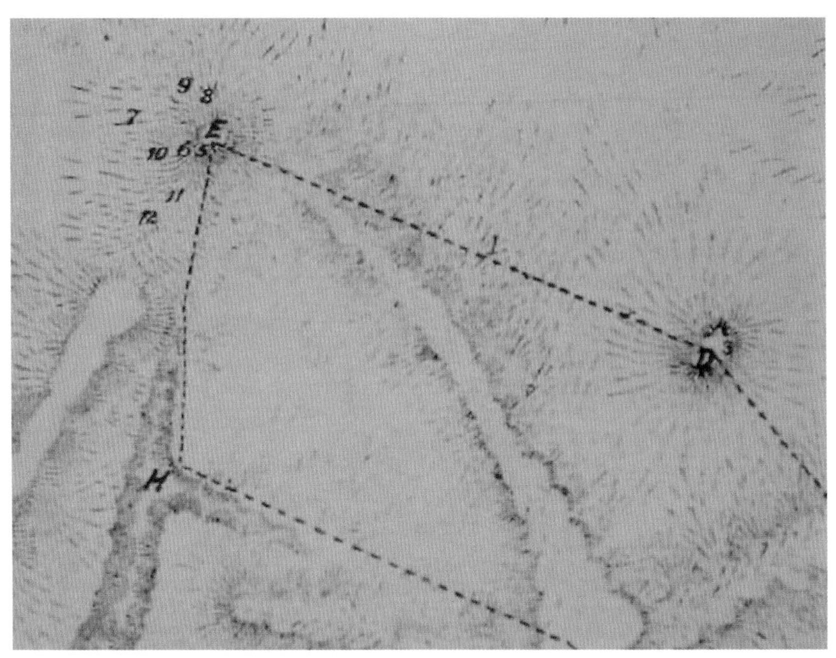
9 8
7
E
10 6 5
11
12
H

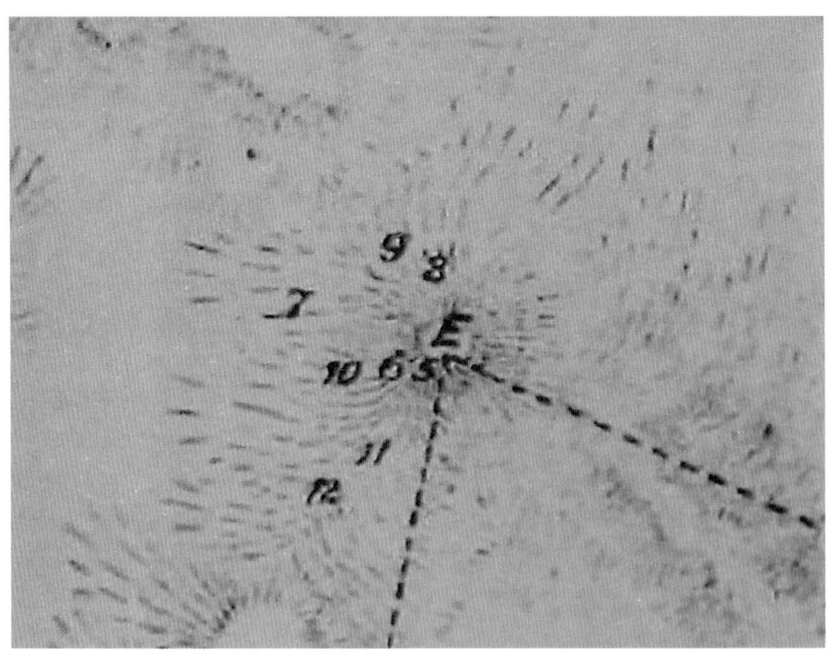
9 8
7
E
10 6 5
11
12

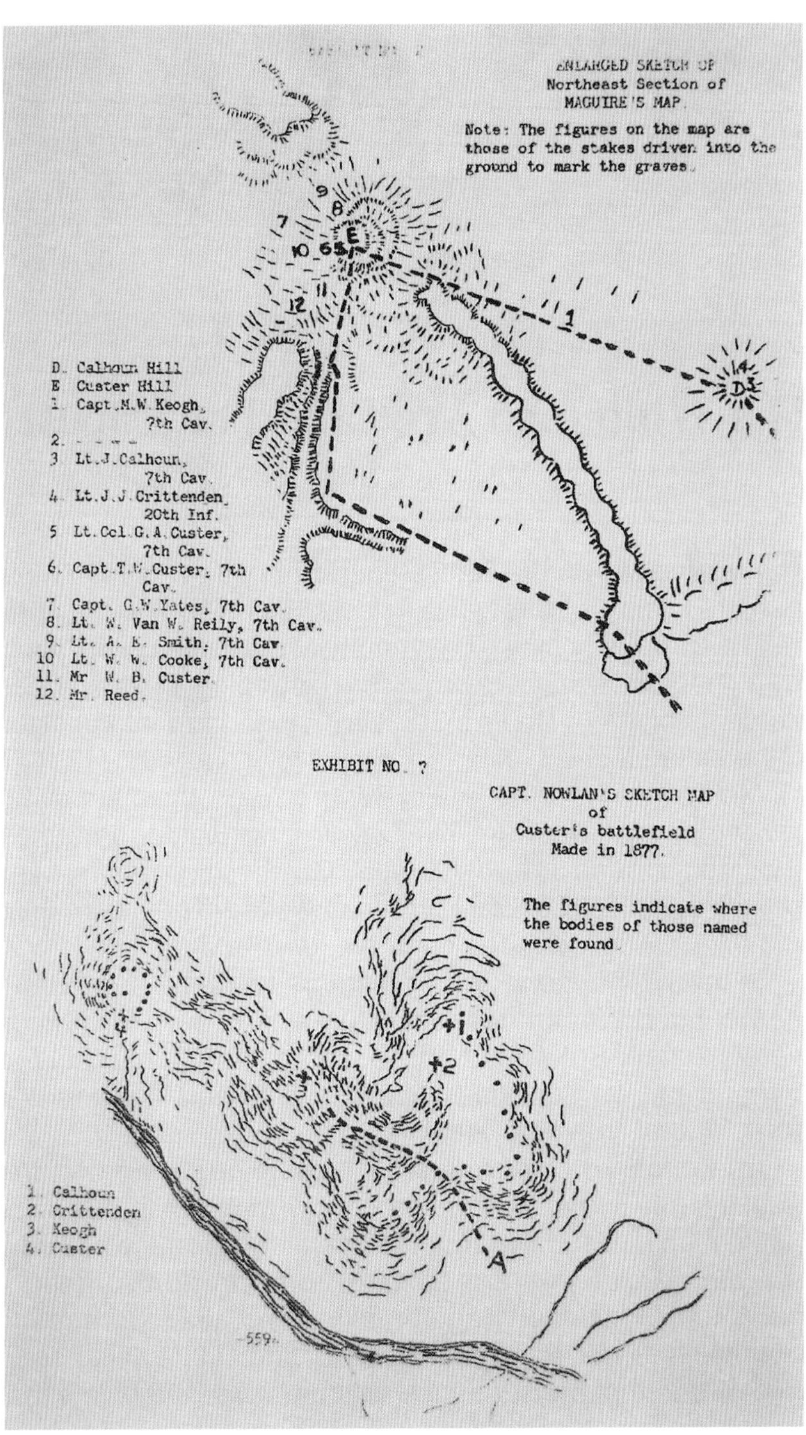
ENLARGED SKETCH OF
Northeast Section of
MAGUIRE'S MAP.
Note: The figures on the map are those of the stakes driven into the ground to mark the graves.
D. Calhoun Hill
E. Custer Hill
1. Capt. M.W. Keogh, 7th Cav.
2. - - - -
3. Lt. J. Calhoun, 7th Cav.
4. Lt. J.J. Crittenden, 20th Inf.
5. Lt. Col. G.A. Custer, 7th Cav.
6. Capt. T.W. Custer, 7th Cav.
7. Capt. G.W. Yates, 7th Cav.
8. Lt. W. Van W. Reily, 7th Cav.
9. Lt. A. E. Smith, 7th Cav.
10. Lt. W. W. Cooke, 7th Cav.
11. Mr. W. B. Custer.
12. Mr. Reed.
EXHIBIT NO. 7
CAPT. NOWLAN'S SKETCH MAP of Custer's battlefield Made in 1877.
The figures indicate where the bodies of those named were found.
1. Calhoun
2. Crittenden
3. Keogh
4. Custer
A
-559-

8

The Whitemen Are Like The Locusts

By sundown on the 25th, General Terry and his men were still twenty to twenty-five miles to the north. The marches had been brutally slow. The mouth of the Little Bighorn still lay a good day's march away. More disturbing, the advanced elements of Major Bribin's 2nd Cavalry had run into hostiles in the distance.

Major Reno and Captain Benteen and their surviving seven companies of the 7th Cavalry had settled into their positions around the low swale. On the high bluffs overlooking the Little Bighorn River they waited. They were tired and thirsty. The wounded cried out for relief.

In the village the returning warriors tended to family and the wounded. As darkness set in, great fires were lit. Dances were initiated. But so too, there was great mourning in the camp. Dead warriors had been brought back to camp and great funeral fires had been lit.

In a circle of chiefs, debate was going on among the tribal elders. Some thought they could wipe out the soldiers on the high bluffs to the south the next day. Some who knew that more soldiers were coming from the north, thought they should have the village break up and head for the Wolf Mountains to the south and west. Sitting Bull, having seen the fulfillment of his sundance vision warned the chiefs that the Indian peoples should not take from the dead white soldiers, or forever become dependent on the whiteman's ways. He knew, as did Inkpaduta, that the words of Chief Little Crow from the Sioux war in Minnesota still held true.

> ***The Whitemen are like the locusts, when they fly so thick that the whole sky is a snowstorm. You may kill one, two, ten, yes as many as the leaves in the forest yonder, and their brothers will not miss them. Kill one, two, ten, and ten times ten will come to kill you. Count your fingers all day long and Whitemen with guns in their hands will come faster than you can count.***

Inkpaduta knew with soldiers coming their way it was time to run once again. Inkpaduta had over nineteen years of experience in evading the bluecoats. He had been evading pursuing troops ever since the Spirit Lake Massacre in 1857. His advice to the chiefs was to head for Canada.

As the looting and mutilation of the dead soldiers continued the next day, Sitting Bull looked around with anger in his heart. "Take nothing belonging to the soldiers. Leave everything here!" But Indian traditions were strong. The spoils of war were there for the taking. The Indian people failed to heed Sitting Bull's exhortations.

Sitting Bull knew of the dangers remaining in the Little Bighorn River valley and began moving his village of Hunkpapa about 6:00 p.m. on the 26th. The soldiers under Major Reno and Captain Benteen watched in amazement at the size of the large Indian village. Camp after camp moved south, away from the approaching Terry-Gibbon column. Some of the soldiers would testify at the Reno Court of Inquiry that the sight looked like a large brown moving mass, about three miles in length and a mile wide. Never again would such a large gathering of Indians be seen roaming the open prairies of the Great Plains.

What did follow was the fulfillment of Little Crow's warning. General Sherman in Washington and Lieutenant- General Sheridan in Chicago began to amass Army units from all over the West. From Texas would come Colonel Ranald Slidell Mackenzie and his 4th Cavalry. Colonel Nelson Miles and his infantry units of the 5th and 22nd Infantry Regiments would move into eastern Montana. General Crook and Colonel Wesley Merritt and his 5th Cavalry would move north to rendezvous with General Terry. This column then began a summer-long pursuit.

As Phil Sheridan had learned with and from his friends and fellow warrior generals, William Tecumseh Sherman and Ulysses S. (Unconditional Surrender) Grant, total war could and would break any foe. Sheridan had once told Count Otto von Bismarck in 1870:

"The proper strategy consists in the first place in inflicting as telling blows as possible upon the enemy's army, and then causing the inhabitants so much suffering that they must long for peace, and force their government to demand it. The people must be left nothing but their eyes to weep with over the war."

Sheridan had explained his strategies for dealing with the hostile Indians to Sherman in 1870:

"I have to select that season when I can catch the fiends; and if a village is attacked and women and children killed, the responsibility is not with the soldiers but with the people whose crimes necessitated the attack. During the (Civil) War did anyone hesitate to attack a village or town occupied by the enemy because women and children were within its limits? Did we cease to throw shells into Vicksburg or Atlanta because women or children were there?"

Vicksburg had been Sherman's and Grant's masterpiece victory in the West to open the Mississippi River to the Union. Sherman had burned Atlanta to the ground and then marched to the sea, burning all in his path. Sheridan had scorched the Shenandoah Valley in Virginia. Grant had destroyed Petersburg and Richmond. Even the masterful tactics of General Robert E. Lee could not stop the sledgehammer approaches of these three Union warriors.

In addition to the total war mentality Sheridan, Sherman, and President Grant had all ascribed to during the Civil War, these men had come to know and appreciate the powerful presence of the expanded railroads. The western commands of the Army, though woefully undermanned compared to the Civil War commands, were far more mobile with the advent of the railroads. Men and supplies could be shunted about the country in a matter of days to meet most any threat. More and more Army posts had been consolidated or closed because the railroads offered such flexibility.

The Indians had seen the many Iron Horses invade the lands of the buffalo. Wherever the Iron Horse made its tracks, the buffalo soon disappeared. So too did the roaming Indian bands dependent on the life giving *pte,* the American bison.

The Army encounters to tame the Indians soon began in earnest for the tribes of Indians present at the Little Bighorn on that June 25 and 26. On July 17, 1876, off reservation Indians in Nebraska on Warbonnet Creek were attacked by the 5th Cavalry of Colonel Wesley Merritt and Lieutenant-Colonel Eugene Carr. They were led by scout Buffalo Bill Cody.

On September 9, 1876, units from General Crook's column in Wyoming and Merritt's recently arrived 5th Cavalry, marched east to Slim Buttes, South Dakota. Here they engaged tribal members of the Minneconjous under American Horse. It was here that the guidon from Captain Keogh's Company I was retrieved. The long march east without proper supplies, had cost the 5th Cavalry most of its horses. The men would eat many of their mounts to stay alive. The march would be known as the "horse-meat march."

Farther north in Montana, Colonel Nelson Miles found Sitting Bull's followers on Cedar Creek. On October 21, 1876 Miles successfully engaged Sitting Bull's warriors. The engagement was brief, and Miles expected to meet Sitting Bull the next day to discuss surrender. However, Sitting Bull and many of his followers used the night to steal away and head for Canada. Miles destroyed all the Indian supplies left behind and prepared for a long winter campaign.

To the south, at the headwaters of the Powder River, Colonel Ranald Mackenzie and his 4th Cavalry found the Northern Cheyenne tribe of Dull Knife. Mackenzie, a favorite of General Grant during the Civil War, had successfully tamed the much-feared Commanche of Quanah Parker in northern Texas the year before. On November 25 and 26, 1876, on the Red Fork of the Powder River, MacKenzie attacked. It was a dreadfully cold winter's day. The 4th Cavalry caught the Cheyennes by surprise. Though the Indians successfully fought a rear guard action to let the village inhabitants flee, most of the Indians' winter supplies were left behind.

Mackenzie's men went through the village belongings and soon found 7th Cavalry equipment. Most telling was the bucksin jacket of Captain Tom Custer and a glove with his initials, "TWC."

The Cheyennes trekked northward through a frightful blizzard to find refuge in the camp of Crazy Horse's Oglalas. The Oglalas would forever remember how poor and weak the Cheyennes looked that winter day as they slowly made their way into the Oglalas' camp.

The actions continued deep into the winter. The winter of 1876 -1877 was to be one of the coldest on record. Deep snows and below zero temperatures were common throughout the northern plains that year. Colonel Nelson Miles, "Bearcoat Miles" as the Indians would call him, was beginning his total war campaign to root out the remaining hostiles of Sitting Bull's and Crazy Horse's camps. In December, the troops under Miles found followers of Sitting Bull first on Bark Creek and then again on Ash Creek in northern Montana. The Hunkpapa split into those who went to Canada to join Sitting Bull, while the rest agreed to head to the reservation. The Sioux tribes at this point were mostly disarmed and too disheartened to fight anymore.

A few hostile tribes remained. One was led by Crazy Horse. He had led his band up the Tongue River. Using Crow scouts, Colonel Miles hunted Crazy Horse and his followers. They were hoping to negotiate a surrender without bloodshed. The Crow scouts, however, attacked and killed the party sent by Crazy Horse to talk peace with Miles. Crazy Horse and his followers sensed that Miles was deceitful in his motives. They fled farther up river. Miles pursued even as the temperatures dropped and the snows deepened.

On January 8, 1877, Miles and his men were confronted by the desperate warriors following Crazy Horse at Wolf Mountain. The Indians outnumbered the troops, but the troops were determined and prepared for a winter fight. By the end of the day, the village was in disarray and much needed winter supplies were destroyed by the Army.

As the harsh winter melted into spring, one engagement remained. A band under Minneconjou Chief Lame Deer had made camp on Muddy Creek, a small tributary to the Rosebud Creek. On May 7, 1877, Colonel Nelson Miles found the village and defeated Lame Deer and his band. With no hope of remaining free on the Plains, the desperate followers of Crazy Horse who escaped Wolf Mountain, surrendered May 8, 1877, at Camp Robinson, in Nebraska. Soon the other remaining bands of roaming Indians were heading to the various Indian Agencies established by the Army. Thus ended the Sioux War of 1876 -1877.

9

Fear, Blood, Making the Past Right

Though the feared Sitting Bull sat in Canada and Crazy Horse was encamped at the Red Cloud Agency by Camp Robinson in Nebraska, troubles remained. Chief Red Cloud, victorious leader of the Sioux in their war against the Army during the years of 1866 to 1868, was the nominally accepted leader of all Plains Indians by the authorities in Washington. General Sherman in seeking to resolve the troubles out West, ordered Red Cloud and all Agency Indian Chiefs to sign and cede away the sacred Paha Sapa (Black Hills) on August 15, 1876. A great controversy began among Indians who had been long on the reservations and agency camps, and the recently arrived defeated non-reservation Indians.

At Camp Robinson and the Red Cloud Agency in Nebraska, trouble became inevitable. Ever since Crazy Horse had surrendered in May, Red Cloud and his close associates had feared the presence of Crazy Horse. Crazy Horse had an aura about him, that even in defeat, stirred Indian passions. An old friend of Crazy Horse, Little Big Man, and his band had allied themselves with Red Cloud while on the Red Cloud Agency.

Perhaps envious of Crazy Horse's instant popularity at the camp, suspicions and plots began. The Army ever sensitive to seeing roaming hostile Indians on the Plains again, kept a close watch on the Indian tensions at Camp Robinson. Washington summoned Crazy Horse to go East, much as leaders in Washington had done with Red Cloud in the late 1860s. Crazy Horse refused, wanting only to be forgotten as a warrior and live free as he had before.

Rumors began at Camp Robinson that Crazy Horse wanted to kill General Crook. First Lieutenant William Clark, the camp commander, worked with Red Cloud's representatives and sought ways to arrest Crazy Horse. They wanted to remove his presence from the boiling situation. With plots and rumors abounding that Crazy Horse would leave the camp and go back to his old ways, the soldiers at Camp Robinson were ordered to arrest Crazy Horse.

The arresting party accompanied by Little Big Man, Crazy Horse's old friend, found Crazy Horse in camp. With Little Big Man's hand tightly grasping Crazy Horse's arm as he approached the camp guard house, Crazy Horse sensed he was being betrayed. He turned to escape. During the commotion, a soldier's bayonet found its way to Crazy Horse's back. During the night of September 5, 1877, Crazy Horse died.

Meanwhile up north, Sitting Bull and Gall had made their escape to Canada after their encounter with Miles. However Gall had a falling out with Sitting Bull, and on January 3, 1881, surrendered at the Poplar River Agency in Montana. He later moved to Standing Rock Reservation. He eventually worked with the government to further the education of his Indian followers. He died at his home on Oak Creek on the reservation in South Dakota in 1894.

In 1880 General Terry was commissioned with negotiating the return of Sitting Bull to the United States. Facing starvation with his followers in Canada, Sitting Bull surrendered at Fort Buford, North Dakota, on July 19, 1881. He and his followers were assigned to the Standing Rock Reservation in 1883.

Buffalo Bill Cody sought out Sitting Bull in 1885 for Cody's famous Buffalo Bill's Wild West show. Reenactments of Custer's Last Stand done in a most showy way portrayed

General Custer as a heroic Indian fighter, being the last of his men to go down before the evil, savage forces of Sitting Bull. Sitting Bull grew tired of the biased whiteman shows and returned to the reservation.

However, much like Crazy Horse had experienced, Indian suspicions grew as to Sitting Bull's power, his medicine, and his intentions for the reservation Indians. Out West, a Paiute medicine man named Wovoka had a death experience while suffering a severe fever. During his dreams, the Great Father Spirit had told him to tell his people how to live and dance so the people could be reunited with the dead. Death would be no more. The white men would forever disappear.

This tribal dance and medicine made its way east to the agencies and reservations of the Sioux. The Ghost Dance of 1890 began to find sway among the starving tribes. With the return of Sitting Bull and the power of the Ghost Dance, suspicions grew among reservation Indians and the Army alike. At the Pine Ridge Agency Camp, Agent James McLaughlin feared another Sioux war. He, therefore, sent an armed guard of agency Indians and soldier guards to arrest and detain Sitting Bull.

On December 15, 1890, in the process of his arrest, Sitting Bull was killed at the hands of his Indian captors. His was buried in South Dakota on the Standing Rock Reservation, though controversary once again followed Sitting Bull. His remains were later claimed to have been stolen and reburied elsewhere.

Tensions were now out of control. The followers of Sitting Bull danced the Ghost Dance in the brutal cold of a northern winter. A band of Minneconjou Sioux under Chief Big Foot had established themselves at a small camp on the Wounded Knee Creek. Agent James McGlaughlin fearing an outbreak of war, summoned the help of the 7th Cavalry, now under the command of Colonel James Forsythe. With Colonel Forsythe rode officers Moylan, Wallace, Varnum, Godfrey, and Edgerly, the very men who had ridden down Reno Creek with General Custer that June 25, 1876.

Late in the day, December 29, 1890, a gunshot rang out, its shooter unknown to all. But remembering the dead of the 7th Cavalry and their mutilated bodies buried there on the hillside of the Little Bighorn River, the guns of the 7th Cavalry sounded with fury and revenge. The Battle of Wounded Knee was a bloody day for the Sioux.

Years later, in February, 1973, Wounded Knee once again became the site for confrontation. The American Indian Movement (AIM) with leaders such as Dennis Banks, Russell Means, and brothers Clyde and Vernon Bellecourt and others were acting in the 1970s to re-establish Indian rights. American Indian treaty rights had been callously forgotten over the decades. At Wounded Knee, AIM occupied for seventy-one days the ground made sacred by the blood of the Sioux on that cold December day in 1890. Included in this gathering of protesters were brothers George and Robert Yellow Bird, grandsons to Monaseetah and, yes, to one George Armstrong Custer.

The U. S. Federal District Court in St. Paul was often the site for confrontation and press reports resulting from the Wounded Knee Indian occupation. Even into the 1970s the fears and the suspicions of red man and white man remained. The blood of fallen families still fighting the long battle of tribal ways versus the white man's ways.

In 1975, two FBI agents were killed at the Pine Ridge Reservation. A contentious murder trial of one Indian, Leonard Peltier, for the death of those FBI agents rekindled the hatreds and fears of white man and red man. Even today, it provokes heated discussion as to who was guilty, and who the victim or victims were at Pine Ridge.

Fears, suspicions, and bloodshed remained, and still remain. Somehow the stories of old still haunt the current day. In 1992, I took my family to visit the grounds of the then Custer Battlefield. No Indian Memorial existed then. Rather, the story still remained that Custer had made a heroic attempt to gain the village and was killed on the Last Stand Hill. He died, being overrun by overwelming numbers of Indians.

As I stated in the opening of this book, some of the facts of June 25,1876, seemed to have been overlooked. Years of fears, suspicions, tainted memories for glorious fallen heroes seemed to have overshadowed how the soldiers fought and died that day. Yes five companies of men died. So too, American Indian blood was shed on that ground. Indian survivors would for years tell of how wounded Indians were laid to rest many days after having made that slow, southerly trek past the soldiers on Reno-Benteen Hill.

When I stood on Calhoun Hill in 1992, a lone American Indian stood near me. He stood silently over the markers where Company L fell, and nearby the one-time actual grave, of Lieutenant John Crittenden. His silent reaction to the marker stood as a powerful reminder to me that the events of that day in June 1876, still affected Americans even to this day. What did that lone American Indian think as he stood there?

All officers who were killed that day were temporarily buried where they fell. The next year, in 1877, families requested reinterment of the officers who were still buried on the battlefield. All were removed, save the missing Lieutenants Harrington, Porter, and Sturgis who were never found, and Lieutenant Crittenden. Lieutenant Crittenden's father had requested that his son remain buried where he fell.

Today, Lieutenant Crittenden, along with Major Reno and Lieutenant William Wyck Van Reilly, lies buried in the National Cemetery located where Yates had his command turned by Crazy Horse and Two Moons and their bands. For Major Reno, he could never escape the lasting impact of Custer's Last Stand, rightly or wrongly.

Lieutenant- Colonel, brevet Major- General, George Armstrong Custer, at the request of his wife, Elizabeth, was buried at West Point. Elizabeth, better known as Libbie, was buried beside her husband in 1933. Captain Myles Keogh was reinterred in his home town in New York at the request of his sister. Likewise, Lieutenant William Cooke was returned to his home in Canada.

After a long, sad return to Fort Leavenworth, Kansas, four officers were laid to rest, side by side. They were Lieutenant James Calhoun, Lieutenant Algernon Smith, Captain George Yates, and the last man standing, two-time Medal of Honor winner, Captain Thomas Ward Custer.

The battle sequence I put together was reconstructed from the testimonies of the Army survivors during the Reno Court of Inquiry held in Chicago in January and February 1879. The testimonies of Trumpeter John Martin, Sergeant Daniel Kanipe, Private Peter Thompson, the Crow Scouts, and the detailed account of Joseph White Cow Bull to David Humphreys Miller all added a clearer understanding of the events of that day.

Most interesting was reconciling the placement of the "gray horse" company, Company E. Along the Reno Creek, Captain Benteen placed it at the rear of Custer's column. This was the last he saw of the Custer column. When Trumpeter Martin last saw the "gray horse" company, it was in the "middle" of the column. When White Cow Bull saw the soldiers attack at the river's edge, he shot two lead men riding gray horses. Therefore, the "gray horse" company had to have been moved forward by Custer to the front, probably along side of Captain Yates' lead battalion company, Company F.

To ford the Little Bighorn River, the troops moved in a column of fours. Reno's troops crossed in column of fours per testimony at the RCOI. Custer's/Yates' troopers would also have done so.

My times are estimated based on the known time that the 7th Cavalry left the Crows Nest on the divide between the Rosebud and the Little Bighorn, which was around noon that day per Lieutenant George Wallace's report. I looked at topographic maps and used a rough estimate of six to eight miles per hour travel time for mounted cavalry at a trot, or twelve to sixteen miles per hour when they moved at a gallop. The distances covered would support the times I put to various actions.

The testimony of the men caught in the timber after Reno's hasty retreat, lended credence to the times of Custer's attack at Ford B. The testimony of Reno's, Benteen's and McDougall's men made clear that volleys were heard at the river's edge downstream and on Nye-Cartwright Ridge. I have those on Nye-Cartwright Ridge as being made by Captain Keogh's men, since the gray horse troops of Captain Yates' battalion were seen leading at the river's edge by White Cow Bull and Bobtail Horse.

Custer was not a fool in his attack. He was rather repeating an attack plan that he had successfully employed at the Battle of the Washita. The difference this time was that he was leading his attack column, the men of Captain Yates' battalion. Custer was shot out of the saddle by White Cow Bull. This occurred while starting to cross the Little Bighorn at the Medicine Tail Coulee Ford. This became Ford B as Lieutenant Edward Maguire would survey it on his map.

General George Custer was zealous and desperate in his need for a noteable victory. He well knew President Grant would be pushing for Custer's court-martial after the debacle in Washington that spring. Custer failed in his not communicating to his subordinates the tactics of how taking and holding the Indian village center would gain the victory, as it had at the Washita.

Once critically wounded, the command structure of the 7th Cavalry worked against any chance of success. With Custer down, the regiment's command belonged to Major Marcus Reno, though even in 1879 at his court of inquiry, he and Captain Benteen did not acknowledge this. What was highlighted at that hearing was the great disdain and lack of confidence Reno and Benteen had in Custer's military abilities. They in no way wished to rush to Custer and the men riding with him.

What they needed to understand but did not was that they as senior commanders of the 7th Cavalry, were responsible for accepting the fate of the soldiers of the entire regiment. This included men under Captain Keogh and Captain Yates as well as the men fighting on Reno-Benteen Hill. Both Major Marcus Reno and Captain Frederick Benteen were admonished by the military board at the Reno Court of Inquiry for not fully complying with the orders given by General George Armstrong Custer. Whether they liked Custer or not, they were still officers of the U.S. Army responsible for the men in the command.

At Ford B and the battle there, Captain Yates as battalion commander of the three companies at the river's edge, should have known that to ride back to the heights of Nye-Cartwright and Captain Keogh's command would have been prudent. Captain Keogh was the senior officer on this end of the battlefield with Major Reno and Captain Benteen absent. By riding east to the heights or south to meet Benteen, Yates would have found a better chance to survive the onslaught of the multitude of warriors.

Likewise Captain Keogh made a mistake in leaving the high ground on Nye-Cartwright by heading north to meet Yates on Calhoun Hill. When confronted with lost initiative, cavalry tactics dictated a hasty retreat from the battlefield on horseback. Cavalry were not trained to fight as infantry. A skirmish interval for cavalrymen was five yards between men to allow for movement of the horses. Infantry fought shoulder to shoulder. With intervals of five yards between the cavalrymen, the superior numbers of Indians could easily penetrate the single shot rifle fire of the soldiers' Springfield carbines.

The markers today on the field show that the command fought as separate companies, not as a single five-company force. Lieutenant Maguire's map showed two lines of retreat from Ford B. One must assume that the one line of retreat closest to the Little Bighorn was that of the soldiers caught on foot. The other line leading to Calhoun Hill was the line of Yates' mounted troops.

Had the horses of Keogh's and Calhoun's men not been spooked and fled, Keogh could have escaped with Company I and Company L to the east before the Indians of Gall had come around the east end of their line on Calhoun Hill. Once the horses were gone and Crazy Horse managed his charge up Crazy Horse Ravine, the two companies waiting with Keogh were easy victims to the large numbers of mounted and unmounted Indians.

Likewise, when Crazy Horse turned Captain Yates and his men on the north end of the battlefield, had Yates continued east past Last Stand Hill an avenue of escape was open. Yates forced the end of his command when he ordered his men to dismount and form a skirmish line.

Had Captains Keogh and Yates not dismounted, but instead rode their commands to the east and then north, either could have survived. They could have met Terry. Or to the south, as the Crow scouts found, Yates and Keogh could have met Reno's and Benteen's battalions. These northern companies could have survived with some of their men. It would have meant sacrificing the men on foot from the Ford B fight. It would have probably sealed the fate of General Custer as well.

As Major Reno had done in his hasty, perhaps panicked, retreat from the valley fight, Captains Keogh and Yates could have saved part of their commands. They would have had to sacrifice those caught in unfortunate circumstances. After all, Reno had abandoned a good portion of Company G and some of Company A in the timber when he rode to Reno-Benteen Hill.

For a moment, Captain Keogh thought he could save everyone on his end of the battlefield. It was a kind thought, a generous thought. It was a thought that killed all his men and those of Yates.

"State whether or not in your opinion, General Custer could have fled the field with a portion of his command by abandoning the others to their fate?"

This key question was asked only once by the Reno Court of Inquiry, and then only to Second Lieutenant Winfield Edgerly, second- in- command of Company D. He was with the Benteen battalion. It was never answered directly.

Lieutenant Edgerly politely responded, "He fought very desperately."

So too did the men who were never mentioned by name at the Reno Court of Inquiry. Attached in the appendix of this book is the list of the dead and missing who rode with the 7th Cavalry that June, 1876.

David Humphreys Miller ascertained through his interviews with the Indian survivors a list of Indians killed at the Little Bighorn. However, as the large village left the valley, many more severely wounded Indians would die. Old She Bear had died a week after the Battle of the Rosebud with General Crook. He was buried in the "lone teepee" that Yates and his troops had set afire on June 25, 1876. Many more teepee lodges would be constructed in the days and weeks after June 25. Those names were known only to the surviving families and bands of Indians. The names of the Indian dead were not written down. The names of Indian participants killed on the Little Bighorn were passed down through family histories.

I would add one additional thought. The Battle of the Little Bighorn was tragic and emotional. White men killed Indian. Indian killed white men. Indian killed Indian. White men killed white men. But tragically, family killed family. Many of the 7th Cavalry were family by blood or marriage. General Custer was also family to the Southern Cheyennes. A more tragic story could not have been scripted as it ultimately unfolded.

10

Epilogue- So What Happened

The Battle of the Little Bighorn became known as Custer's Last Stand. The field upon which the body of Lieutenant-Colonel George Armstrong Custer was found was known as the Custer Battlefield for many years. It was not until 1991 that Congress changed the name of the battlefield and the efforts of the Indian participants were formally acknowleged. A new Indian Memorial was erected and located near the markers of Last Stand Hill.

The General of the Army, General William Tecumseh Sherman, and his primary subordinate, Lieutenant- General Philip Sheridan, had planned a campaign during the year of 1876. This campaign was to rid the plains of hostile Indian actions against the railroad survey crews and the settlers who were following the completion of railways across the northern plains. The first actions took place along the Powder River in March, 1876. The larger campaign involving General Crook's column from Wyoming and the Terry-Custer-Gibbon columns began in May, 1876. General Crook encountered the hostile Indians first, on the Rosebud River on June 17, 1876. This was a week before the other columns became engaged.

Custer was under pressure from his superiors, namely his commander-in-chief, President Grant, because of his testimony before Congress that spring. Custer testified about corruption by Army post traders. Custer named Grant's brother, Orvil, as having been involved. President Grant, furious about the matter, informed Sherman and Sheridan that Custer was not to be a part of the summer campaign. Custer tried to appeal to Grant but was refused a meeting at the White House. He left Washington, without orders, for his regiment at Fort Lincoln. Grant then had Custer placed under military arrest.

General Terry knowing his limitations as an Indian fighter, insisted on having Custer lead the 7th Cavalry. This after after Custer had pleaded his case with Terry. Custer would go, but he was still under military arrest, awaiting a probable court-martial at the end of the campaign. Sergeant Daniel Kanipe mentioned the fact that Custer was under military arrest in an interview in 1924.

The column left Fort Lincoln in May without much happening, except for a snowstorm encountered in late May per Lieutenant Edward Maguire's report. Terry sent Major Reno on a scout of the Powder River with six companies. Reno eventually found the trail of the Indians near the Rosebud River. Custer was worried by the selection of Reno to lead the scout instead of himself.

Custer needed the glory of a victory to face his superiors after the campaign. A Custer victory over the Indians would have the newspapers' attention. President Grant would have been hard-pressed to see a court-martial proceed.

As Terry and Gibbon had not found the Indian encampent on the Rosebud, Powder or Tongue rivers, it was surmised that the Indians were somewhere on the Little Bighorn or Bighorn rivers. Terry split his command and gave Custer orders to ride to the head of the Rosebud and then cross to the Little Bighorn. This was in hopes of creating a pincer movement with the Indians between the Gibbon column and Custer's men. The orders anticipated action on June 26.

However both columns found the going took longer than was anticipated. Terry and Gibbon would need an extra day due to the hard terrain even with long marches. They did not arrive on the battlefield until June 27.

Custer seeing the terrain along the Rosebud getting rougher by the mile with the Wolf Mountains in his view, began to question the necessity of proceding to the headwaters of the Rosebud or Tongue. His Crow and Arikara Indian scouts had found the Indian trail leading from the Rosebud to the Little Bighorn. This trail followed current-day Davis Creek.

Custer knowing his orders assumed a fight on the 26th , with Terry's column closing in from the north, pushed his men the night of June 24. Custer felt he would need to scout the Indian encampent on the 25th before trying a morning attack on the 26th. This was Custer's plan per Lieutenant Wallace in his report.

Custer, thinking how he had attacked and gained glory at the Battle of the Washita in November, 1868, planned on assaulting the Indian encampent from as many directions as the terrain would allow. As he had done at the Washita, Custer would divide his command into battalions of three companies each. He left one company with the slow moving pack-train.

As Custer scouted the Little Bighorn valley from the Crow's Nest mountain on the divide between the Rosebud and the Little Bighorn, his plan still seemed doable. However, that morning of the 25th, his column was spotted by a number of different Indian parties. The plan to scout on the 25th and attack on the morning of the 26th was no longer feasible. Custer feared the Indian encampent would soon disperse. Custer's chance for redemption would flee with the Indians.

Therefore at noon on the 25th, Custer assigned his companies to four battalions. Major Reno would lead one, Captain Benteen would lead another, and Captains Keogh and Yates would lead the other two. Custer retained these last two battalions as his main attack force. Custer had kept the largest battalion for his charge as he had done at the Washita.

Not having an exact fix on the location of the village, Custer sent Benteen and his three companies on a scout/

attack to the southwest. Custer was probably thinking that Benteen would be able to attack the south end of the Indian village. He ordered Major Reno and his three companies to move rapidly down the Reno/Ash Creek valley. Reno was to attack and "pitch into" any Indians in his front. Custer probably thought Reno would be at the Indian village center.

Custer veered to the north with his five companies. When upon the high ground of current-day Sharpshooter Ridge, he could finally see the village was located farther north than he had anticipated. He sent messages/orders to retrieve Benteen and the pack-train to join him near the north end of the village.

As Reno and his men engaged the village at about 2:30 p.m., Custer observed some of the valley fight from the high bluffs across the river. Custer moved his men farther north to the vantage point of current Weir Point. This was the highest point from which to see the entire village, per Captain Benteen's observations later.

With a final understanding of the village location and size, Custer probably planned to assault the center of the village located at the Medicine Tail Coulee, later Ford B designation. Most likely Custer planned an attack time around 3:30 p.m. By then Benteen should have been able to move north to be given attack instructions by Captain Keogh. Keogh would wait for him on Nye-Cartwright Ridge.

Custer attacked, leading the Yates battalion, reinforced with the transferred Company C from the Keogh battalion. Things looked winable in Custer's eyes at 3:30 p.m. when he attacked with Captain Yates and his battalion.

Reno had the majority of Indians engaged at the south end of the village. The center of the village appeared deserted. Captain Benteen should have arrived within fifteen to twenty minutes with his three companies. Custer planned to have him strike the north end of the village.

When Captain McDougall arrived with the pack-train, Captain Keogh would come with his men and McDougall's to the center of the village to reinforce Custer's grip there. This is how Custer had fought at the Washita.

However, at 3:20 p.m. things had begun to unravel. Reno's attack had lost the initiative and was in full retreat. Captain Benteen instead of "being quick" had decided to have his command move slowly. Benteen himself went out of the way to check out what was happening in the valley at the Reno Ford A.

As Custer approached the Little Bighorn River at the Medicine Tail Coulee, Ford B, everything changed in a single shot. White Cow Bull, an Oglala Indian, along with a handful of warriors had set up a quick defence in a draw across the river from Custer's approach. White Cow Bull with his repeating rifle felled Custer as well as Lieutenant Algernon Smith, the commander of Company E, the gray horse company.

Custer's battle was over at this point. He went first. He was shot and critically wounded, among the first casualties of the northern battles.

The command situation for the 7th Cavalry was confused at this point. Major Reno, in full retreat at that moment, was the nominal head of all the 7th Regiment with Custer down. However, Reno did not know this.

Captain Yates became commander of Custer's attack with his battalion at the Ford B. Yates made the critical move to first dismount and form a skirmish line while they retrieved the wounded Custer. With Custer retrieved, Dr. Lord pronounced his chest wound critical and in need of the ambulance with Terry to the north. Yates decided to ride to the high ground to his right and rear, now known as Calhoun Hill.

Captain Keogh, not seeing Benteen anywhere in sight and seeing Yates wave him over to Calhoun Hill, left the heights of Nye-Cartwright. Keogh met Yates for an update. Captain Keogh, being the ranking officer at this site, commanded Yates to take the wounded Custer and the civilian Custer family members to General Terry's column. In Captain Keogh's and Adjutant Lieutenant Cooke's estimation, Terry's column should have been twenty to thirty miles to the north if Terry was to be at the battlefield by the 26th.

Captain Yates rode off with his company and that of Company E and the wounded Lieutenant Smith to the north. The Indian survivors recalled seeing the troopers separate on Calhoun Hill.

Captain Keogh knew Benteen should have been on the other side of Weir Point at that moment. Benteen should have been able to reinforce Keogh in a short amount of time. Keogh had his men fight on foot in a skirmish line while they waited for Benteen's arrival.

Keogh ordered Lieutenant Harrington, now in charge of Company C, to support the men on foot from the Ford B fight. Captain Tom Custer was to ride with Yates and the Custer family. The initiative for attack had been lost, but a defence of Calhoun Hill seemed reasonable at that moment.

However, the battle turned on two important moves by the Indians. Those under Gall's direction managed to spook the horses of Company I and Company L. Thus Keogh and his men were forced to fight on foot. They did not have a way to retreat on horseback. At the same time, the warriors of Crazy Horse and Two Moons turned Captain Yates and his men. The Indians at that point had successfully sealed off the avenues of retreat for the five companies. In addition, Indians of the Southern Cheyennes led by Lame White Man came over the top of Battle Ridge and hit Company I from the rear. Crazy Horse and his Ogalas attacked the front.

The warriors with Crazy Horse and Two Moons headed up the ravine behind the current monument to the 7th Cavalry. They saw the exposed cavalrymen of Company I. These Indians rode up and destroyed the companies of Captain Keogh and Lieutenant James Calhoun and his Company L. The end was inevitable.

Below Battle Ridge on Greasy Grass Ridge, the men of Company C panicked. They saw large numbers of Indians emerge on Calhoun Hill after their battalion comrades were wiped out. On someone's command they began a mass suicide. Captain Yates was then the ranking officer left on the northern battlefield.

Captain Benteen finally arrived to see Reno's men on top of the bluff to the south. Major Reno ordered Benteen to stop and support Reno's men. They waited for Captain McDougall and the pack-train to arrive which took another forty-fiv e minutes.

By this time, Yates and his battalion were fighting a desperate fight. Yates had his Company F circle their horses and shoot them to provide a barricade for the men. Captain Tom Custer and First Lieutenant William Cooke stood with Captain Yates. On the ground lay the wounded Lieutenant Algernon Smith and the critically wounded Lieutenant-Colonel George Custer.

Second Lieutenant Sturgis was in charge of the gray horse company, Company E. Sturgis and his men met their end in the Deep Ravine down from the hill, now known as Last Stand Hill.

With the Indians having eliminated the Keogh battalion, the Indians closed in from the north and the south on the men of the Yates battalion. The officers with Yates stood their ground. They desperately yelled at their men to keep shooting. One by one the men fell. One by one the officers fell. First Cooke, then Yates, then Smith, then finally, only one was left standing on that hill.

Captain Thomas Ward Custer, two-time Medal of Honor winner, stood fearless and alone. Wearing his buckskin uniform with the silver bars on his shoulder, tears falling from his eyes as Cheyenne warriors later recalled, Captain Custer had to administer the final shot to the temple of his brother George. He had watched his younger brother Boston, and his nephew Autie Reed get cut down as they ran for their lives. He had witnessed his brother-in-law James Calhoun and his good friend Myles Keogh go down with their companies. To his horror he had watched his men of Company C commit mass suicide.

Custer's Last Stand was to become a metaphor for the glory of George Armstrong Custer and his men. It was a terrible end, but George Armstrong Custer was not cognizant of the horror about him. If one needs to have a Custer as the last hero on that hill, then it would be Captain Thomas Ward Custer. Then indeed it was a Custer's Last Stand.

As for Lieutenant- Colonel, brevet Major- General, George Armstrong Custer, his battle had ended much earlier at Ford B. As Custer himself wrote in his *My Life On The Plains,* he would lead his attacks. He would find either victory or he would die leading a dashing and daring cavalry charge. At the Little Bighorn, George Armstrong Custer led the way. At the Medicine Tail Coulee, while crossing the Little Bighorn River, Custer was shot out of the saddle of his horse, Vic.

The men of five companies of the 7th Cavalry died that day on the northern Yates-Keogh battlefields. Many American Indian warriors were killed or wounded and later died. The battles of the Little Bighorn were tragic for all. White men and Indians killing each other in a clash of cultures and lifestyles. Family killed family. Of the officers of the 7th Cavalry who fought on the northern Keogh-Yates battlefields that June 25, 1876, Captains Myles Keogh and George Yates made a series of decisions that led to their defeats. Captain Thomas Ward Custer made a battle of it with a Custer's Last Stand. Lieutenant- Colonel, brevet Major-General, George Armstrong Custer, however while leading his men at Ford B, went first.

11

Author's Photos

From the southern Reno-Benteen battlefield, looking north, many troopers recalled the "high hill" seen to the right. This hill became known as Sharpshooter Ridge. Custer stopped his column on that hill and went to the edge of the bluffs on the left to witness the Reno valley fight. Captain Keogh and Lieutenant Cooke went with Custer to the edge. Sergeant Kanipe left from this high hill with his message for the pack-train. Trumpeter Martin and privates Thompson and Watson recalled the stop on the "high hill." Kanipe recalled that Yates' troops came up from the lone teepee burning and met Custer here. The gray horse company of Company E was seen to the left of this hill from below.

From this spot, Custer looked on the valley fight below. The valley is to the left of this photo. Custer's column then rode north toward the next "high hill," Weir Point. Captain Benteen said it was the only point from which to see the whole of the Indian village. Trumpeter Martin said Custer, his brother Tom, and nephew Autie Reed went to the top. The column went into the low ground now known as Cedar Coulee on its way to Medicine Tail Coulee. Weir Point is also where Sitting Bull placed his medicine bags the night before the battle.

This is the marker denoting where Sergeant James Butler of Company L was found. It is near the Medicine Tail Coulee ford. Sergeant Butler was shot here as he tried to escape the Yates-Keogh fights. He was trying to deliver the desperate message from Captain Keogh. Survivors recalled finding the first body of Custer's column a few hundred yards from the Little Bighorn River, at the Medicine Tail Coulee. Corporal Foley's marker is located two hundred yards closer to the ford from this marker.

The dark marker denotes where the body of Lieutenant-Colonel George Custer was found. This is now called Last Stand Hill. In the upper left of this photo is the Deep Ravine where Company E met its fate. Most of the near markers belong to Company F and the six officers who died on Last Stand Hill.

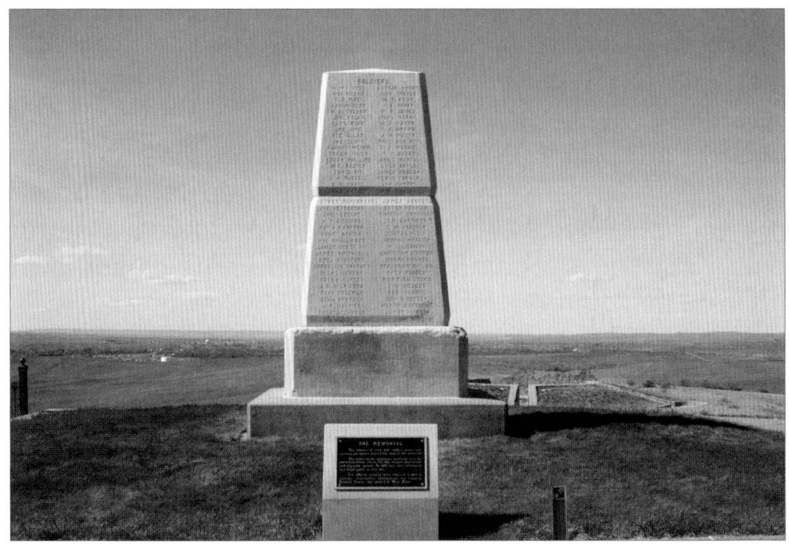

This is the monument to the men of the 7th Cavalry who died at the Little Bighorn. Beneath this monument lie the remains of many of the troopers. The remains of the officers were reinterred elsewhere per family requests.

What was he thinking? On Calhoun Hill I watched this lone American Indian walk among the markers of Company L. In the background, on the distant hill, is the Last Stand Hill monument to the troopers. The low ground to the right of Last Stand Hill, in the center of the picture, is the ravine Crazy Horse and his warriors followed in the attack on Captain Keogh's Company I. The Company I markers are over the hill on which this American Indian is standing, in a line leading to Last Stand Hill.

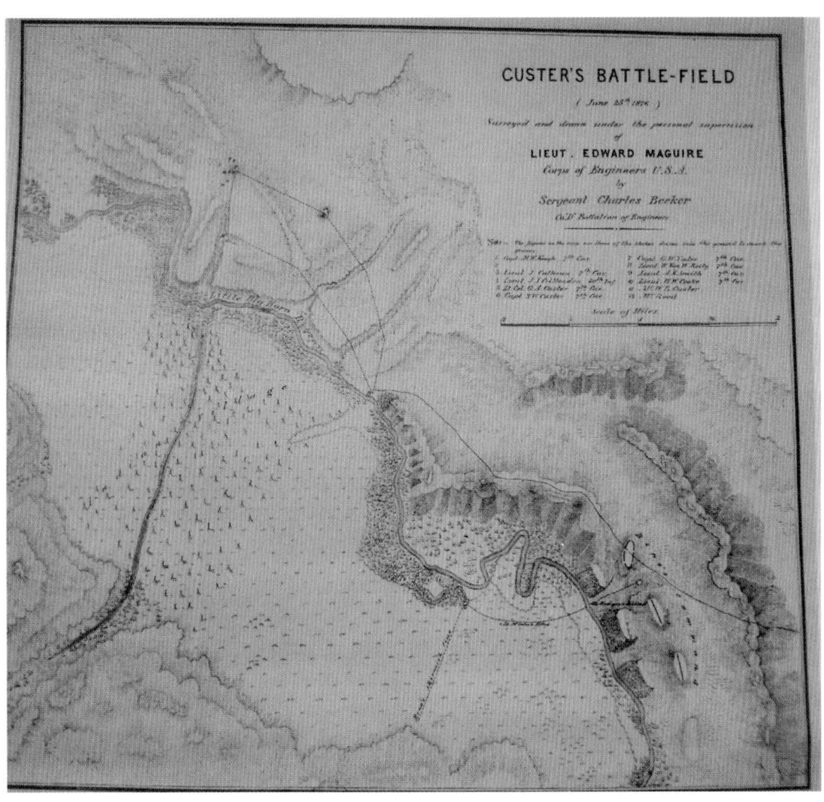

The Maguire map that Lieutenant Maguire and his men prepared for his report.

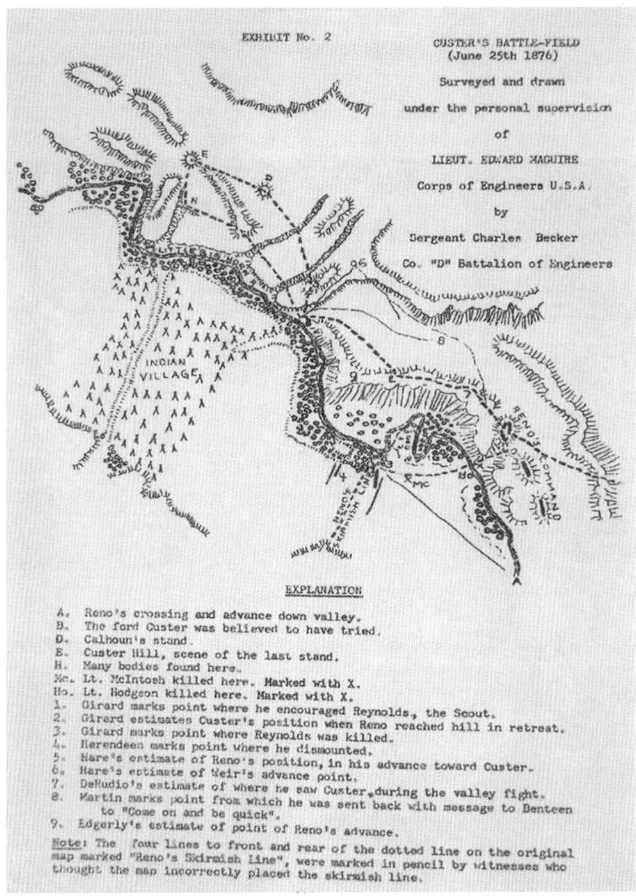
EXHIBIT No. 2

CUSTER'S BATTLE-FIELD
(June 25th 1876)

Surveyed and drawn
under the personal suoervision
of
LIEUT. EDWARD MAGUIRE
Corps of Engineers U.S.A.
by
Sergeant Charles Becker
Co. "D" Battalion of Engineers

EXPLANATION

A. Reno's crossing and advance down valley.
B. The ford Custer was believed to have tried.
D. Calhoun's stand.
E. Custer Hill, scene of the last stand.
H. Many bodies found here.
Mc. Lt. McIntosh killed here. Marked with X.
Ho. Lt. Hodgson killed here. Marked with X.
1. Girard marks point where he encouraged Reynolds, the Scout.
2. Girard estimates Custer's position when Reno reached hill in retreat.
3. Girard marks point where Reynolds was killed.
4. Herendeen marks point where he dismounted.
5. Hare's estimate of Reno's position, in his advance toward Custer.
6. Hare's estimate of Weir's advance point.
7. DeRudio's estimate of where he saw Custer, during the valley fight.
8. Martin marks point from which he was sent back with message to Benteen to "Come on and be quick".
9. Edgerly's estimate of point of Reno's advance.

Note: The four lines to front and rear of the dotted line on the original map marked "Reno's Skirmish Line", were marked in pencil by witnesses who thought the map incorrectly placed the skirmish line.

The Maguire map as marked up at the Reno Court of Inquiry.

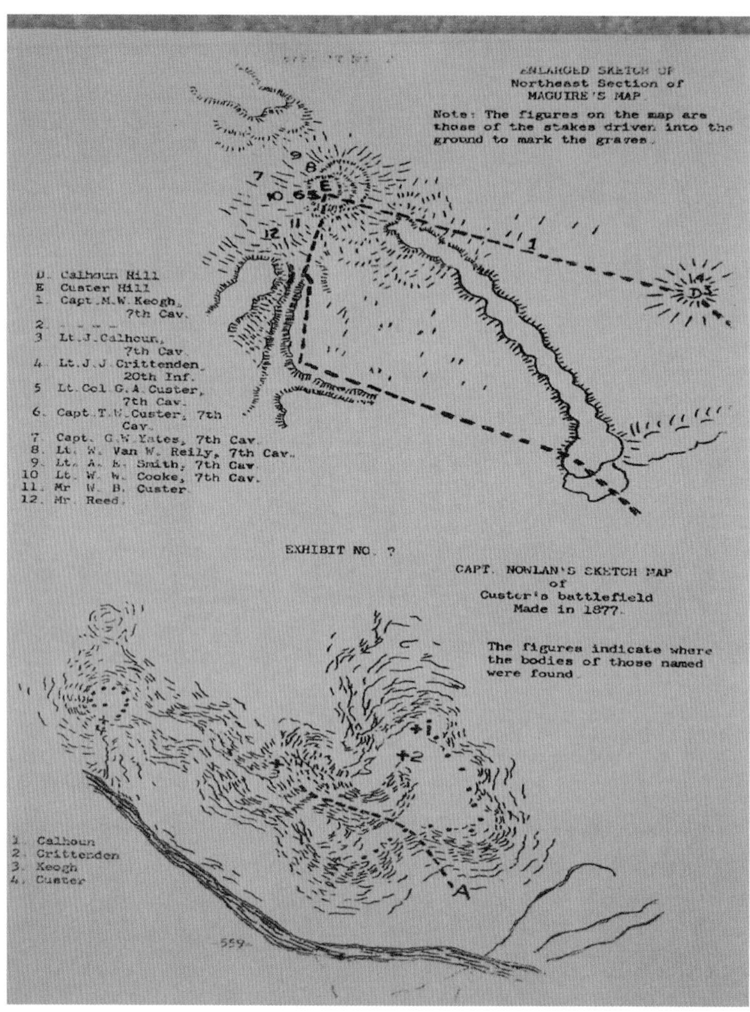

The Maguire map and the Captain Nolan sketch of where Custer's men were found as presented at the Reno Court of Inquiry.

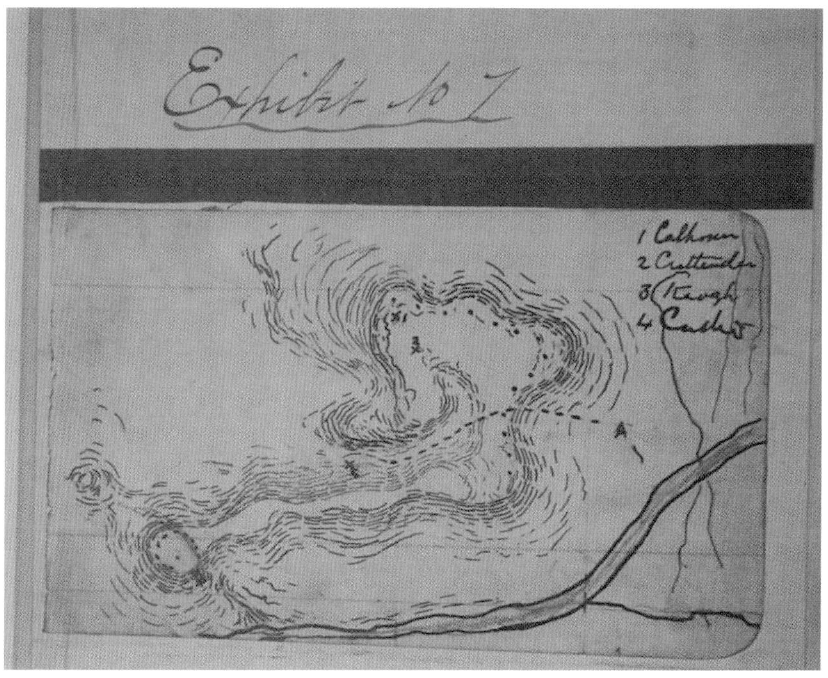

The 1877 sketch by Captain Nolan of where he found bodies.

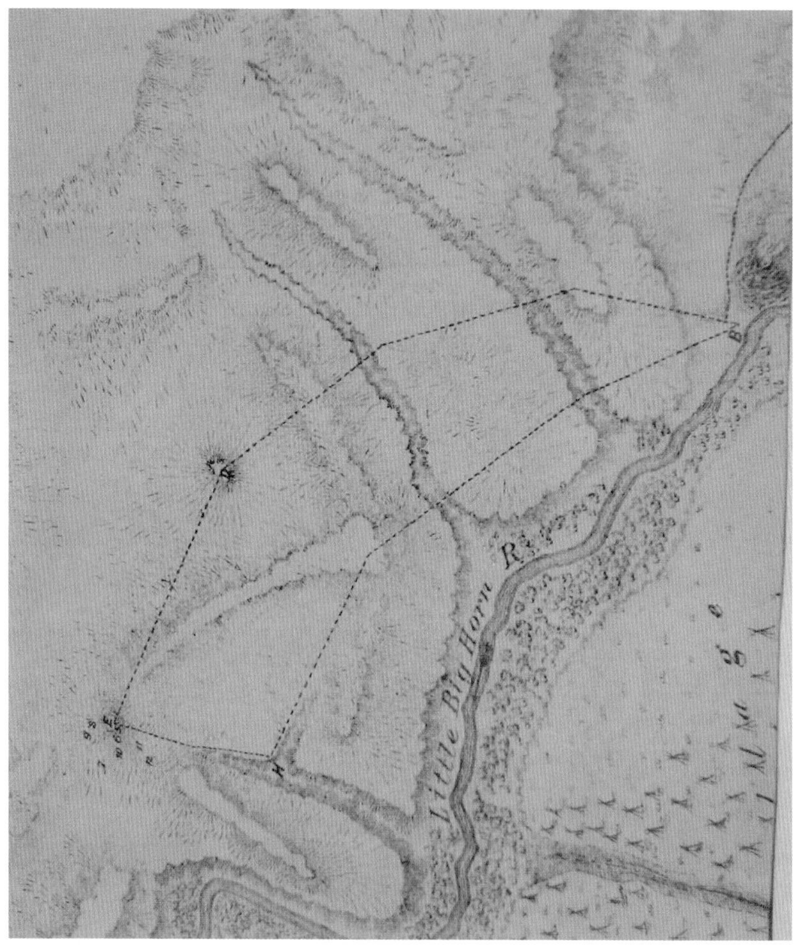

Lieutenant Maguire's map of the northern battlefields. Calhoun Hill is D, the Deep Ravine is H, and E designates Last Stand Hill. "B" designates the Medicine Tail Coulee ford.

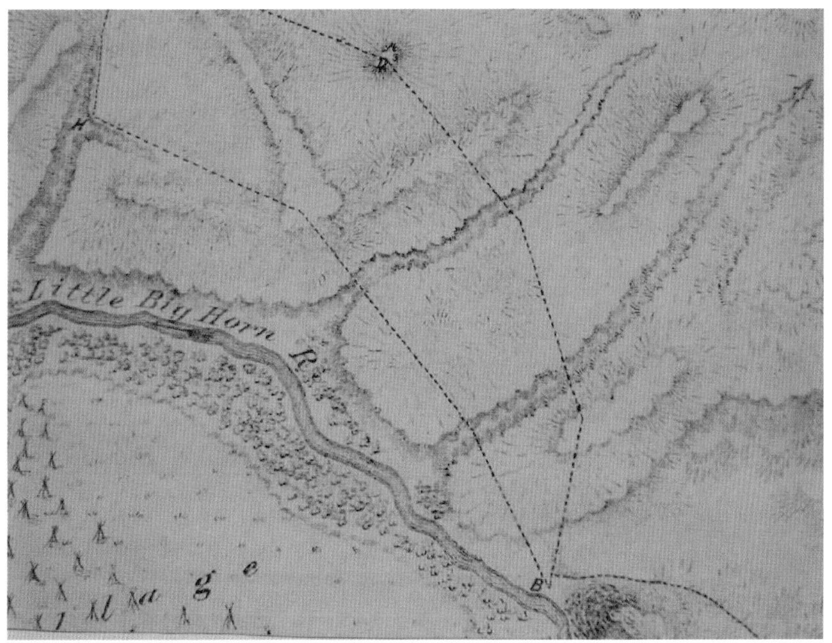

From the Maguire map, note the two paths of retreat from B. Lieutenant Maguire and others noted this observation when searching the battlefield. The RCOI ignored this observation. Private Thompson was to the right of B and witnessed the retreat.

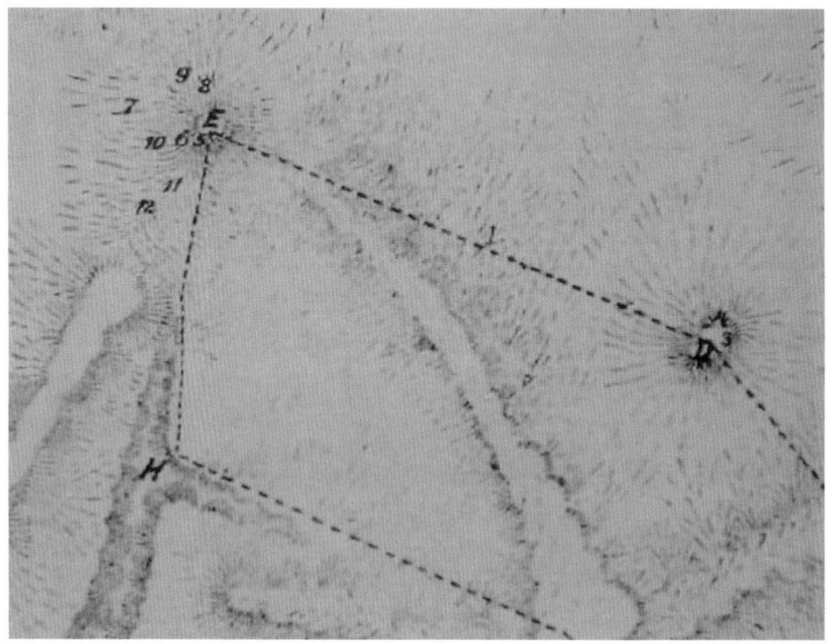

From the Maguire map, company locations were D on Calhoun Hill for Company L, H in the Deep Ravine for Company E, and E on Last Stand Hill for Company F. Captain Keogh was found at 1, Lieutenant Calhoun at 4, and Lieutenant Crittenden at 3. Company I was in line from 1 to D.

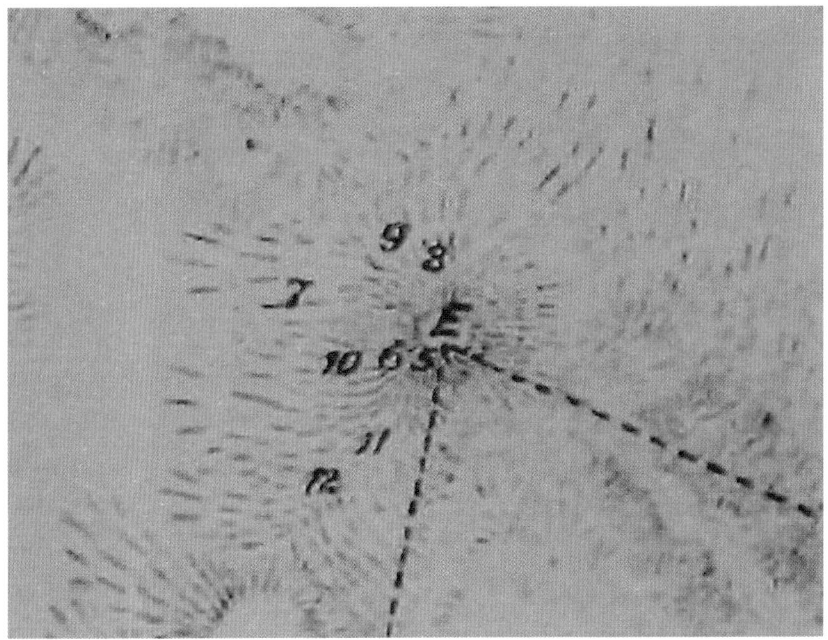

From the Maguire map, positions of the officers found on Last Stand Hill. Lieutenant- Colonel Custer designated as 5. Others are Captain Custer as 6, Lieutenant Cooke as 10, Captain Yates as 7, Lieutenant Smith as 9, Lt. Reilly as 8, Boston Custer as 11 and Autie Reed as 12.

USGS aerial photos of the Little Bighorn battlefields. Reno Creek is the left-right creek in the center.

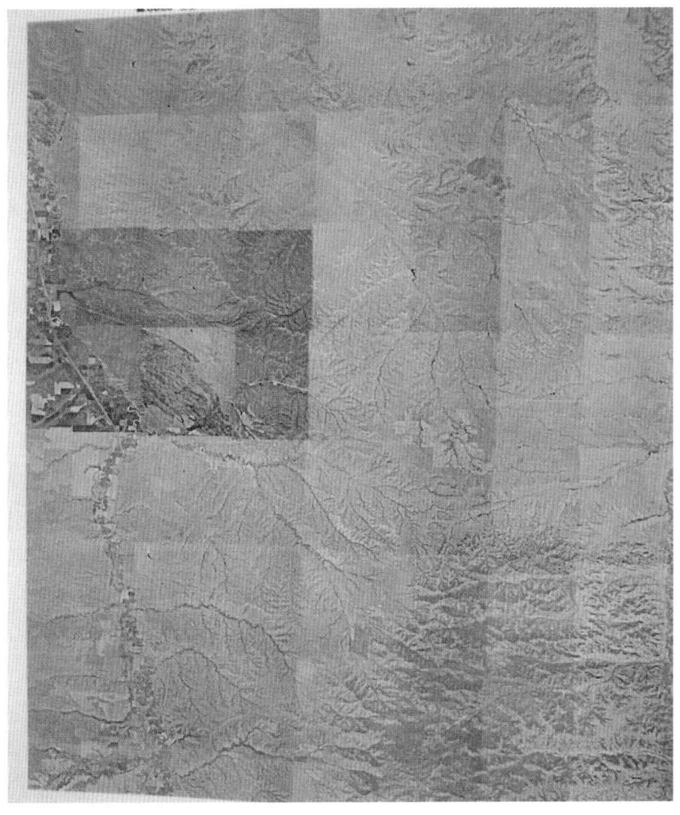

USGS photos showing the Little Bighorn River, Reno Creek, and Davis Creek.

12

April, 2016

It had been almost twenty-four years. It was time to return. In April of 2016, I decided to return to the Little Bighorn. I had been in communication with the National Park Service arranging a week long study of the battlefield. I knew that before publishing my book, my conclusions needed to be verified against the layout of the battlefield and surrounding areas. I had a hunch as to the location of the still missing twenty-eight troopers of Company E lost in the Deep Ravine.

I live in the Twin Cities of Minnesota. My journey would start with a drive from my home to the starting point of the Custer expedition, Fort Lincoln, North Dakota. I arrived a little after noon to find a quiet park. After paying the five dollar daily fee, I parked the car and proceeded to walk the wooden pathway of the old cavalry post. The Commandant's House, known as the Custer House, is the first major structure to catch one's eye. Maintained much as it looked when George and Libby Custer lived there in 1876, one can peer through the windows and see some of the setting as it must have looked to the Custers.

In front of the house is the open space of the parade grounds. Surrounding the parade grounds in a rectangular layout are the foundation cornerstones of the old barracks and post buildings. Directly across from the Custer House is a barracks structure, restored as it would have been to the troopers in 1876.

I walked around the structure and peered through the windows, as in April, the park does not have these structures open to the public. Still, I could see the bunks, the stoves, the tables that would have been filled with the young and old troopers of the 7th Cavalry.

Knowing that the troopers of five companies never returned home to their post, I decided to take a garden trowel and take a couple of scoops of soil from around the barracks and place the dirt in a bag. It would serve as a mission reminder for me later on my journey.

There is a marker immediately north of the parade grounds that denotes the departure point for Custer's column. The slow rise to the right of the marker is the trail where the troopers' journey started.

Leaving Fort Lincoln, I travelled Interstate 94 to Montana. The freeway follows much of the trail the 7th Cavalry rode in 1876. Eventually, I arrived at the juncture of the Yellowstone River and Rosebud Creek. It is here where my journey took to the roads that closest followed the fateful trail of the Custer column.

The Rosebud Creek is a small creek that intersects the Yellowstone River at this riverbend.

From this point, Montana State Highway 447 heads south. The land along this highway is largely unchanged from how it looked in 1876. About twelve miles south from the Yellowstone River, the Custer column made it first camp.

The valley is open and the Rosebud Creek is a meandering waterway. In this area the troops camped on June 22, after leaving the Yellowstone River. The roadside marker had its metal plaque missing, but the stone marker remains.

About forty-two miles from the Yellowstone River, a second stone marker, again the metal plaque was missing, denoted where the column camped on June 23.

The roads change near Lame Deer and Busby. Montana Highway 39 and U.S. Highway 212 lead through the Northern Cheyenne community on the way to the Davis Creek area. Taking Montana Highway 314 a couple of miles south, I tried taking East Reno Creek Road west to the battlefield. The East Reno Creek road soon ended abruptly in a rancher's herd of cattle. I retreated back to Hwy. 314.

Had I taken Hwy 314 south approximately fifteen to twenty miles, I would have come across the Rosebud Battlefield site, but my journey was focused on the movements of the 7th Cavalry, and hence I turned north. I resumed my trek along Hwy 212 to the west. This road intersects Interstate 90 on the northern edge of the Little Bighorn Battlefield. I had travelled close to eighty miles since leaving the Yellowstone River.

One of my first stops upon arrival was the Custer Battlefield Museum, in Garryowen. This museum is located on the site of the Reno valley fight. It was here I met Chris Kortlander. He was busy writing an obituary for legendary Crow Chief Joseph Medicine Crow. Chief Medicine Crow was 102 years old at his death. His grandmother's brother was none other than White Man Runs Him, Custer's scout.

Chris and I had a good discussion about my planned visit. He offered that I join the Custer Battlefield Preservation Committee. This private organization maintains a number of properties adjacent to the National Park properties. Much of the battle occurred on these properties. To obtain permission to explore these lands, I needed a map supplied by the committee and permission from the committee's, Mr. James Court, before any explorations could be made. I thanked Chris for his invaluable help. I then headed to Hardin, Montana, to find a motel for the week I had coming up.

The next day, Monday April 4, I began my visit to the Little Bighorn National Battlefield. Here I was met by Park Ranger Gerald Jasmer. Jerry and I had been exchanging notes regarding my visit beforehand. Jerry was extremely helpful in getting me started.

As it so happened, James Court was in visiting the visitor center when I was there that morning. I explained the purpose of my visit and showed him the map I had from Chris Kortland. Jim was extremely kind in affording me the opportuinty to walk the committee's properties. Jerry Jasmer said it was most fortunate that Jim was there to provide me this opportunity.

I spent a good morning with Jerry explaining my book and its premise. Jerry's expertise of over forty years regarding the battle was extraodinarily helpful in his understanding of my premise. All during the next week, he and the visitor center staff were most welcoming and helpful in guiding me. Though Jerry and the staff have heard numerous versions of the battle, they were kind enough to hear me out. They were most helpful, providing me access to staff when I needed help.

As the battlefield is under the protection of the National Park Service, it is unlawful to walk off the prepared paths for visitors. I needed a special permit with a detailed explanation of which areas I specifically wanted to photograph and walk. Chief Ranger Michael Stops was most helpful in guiding me through this process. When the permit was granted, he authorized Park Rangers Ken Woody and Jerry Jasmer to assist me. As it turned out Jerry would be my guide and escort.

While waiting for the permit processing, I turned my attention to the vast areas of the battle. On Monday I drove to the Reno-Benteen site to survey the area. From here I drove back along the park's road and stopped several times to scope out my research areas. I paid special attention to Sharpshooter Ridge and Weir Point. These were the "high hills" referenced so often in the Reno Court of Inquiry.

View of Sharpshooter Ridge from near Weir Point.

View of Weir Point from the park road near Sharpshooter Ridge.

The grave of White Man Runs Him.

On Tuesday, April 5, I focused on the Custer National Cemetery and stayed close to the visitor center. The weather was poor that day with extreme winds and rain. I completed my permit application. I then walked the cemetery to find notable headstones. I was surprised to find the headstones of Custer's Indian scouts, White Man Runs Him, Curly, and Goes Ahead, Major (brevet Brigadier- General) Marcus Reno, and the headstones of Captains Fetterman and Brown of the famous Fetterman massacre.

The grave of Goes Ahead.

The grave of Curly.

The grave of Captain Fetterman.

The grave of Major (brevet Brigadier- General) Reno.

On Wednesday, April 6, I drove the West Reno Creek Road as far as I could toward the Crows Nest area. I took note of odometer readings as I went. I was able to find the famous watering hole/-morass, which is still as it was then. Today a small bridge crosses the water as the road turns toward the bluffs of Davis Creek. It was here that Captain Benteen's troops rejoined the trail of Reno's and Custer's men after his "valley hunting infinitum."

This is the morass. It is 3.4 miles by odometer reading to Ford A from here.

This is the area of Ford A, the Reno crossing. The high hill in the center is Sharpshooter Ridge. Captain Keogh and Lieutenant Cooke rode up the heights to find Custer viewing the Reno fight from the high ground to the left of Sharpshooter Ridge. This is the area from which Captain Benteen viewed the valley fight. Nearby, Benteen found the Crow scouts and then rode to meet Reno at the Reno-Benteen site. Upon completing my drive of Reno Creek Road, I returned to the battlefield and went to the Ford B, Medicine Tail Coulee. I wanted to see the Sergeant Butler and Corporal Foley markers.

Corporal John Foley's marker, nearest the Ford B.

Sergeant James Butler marker, two hundred yards up a slope from Corporal Foley, near Ford B.

Sergeant Butler marker with Weir Point in background. Corporal Foley's marker is down the slope to the right of this picture view.

These markers were on the properties of the Custer Battlefield Preservation Committee near the Medicine Tail Coulee, also known as Ford B. I took readings from my map compass and a laser range finder. I determined that Lieutenant Maguire used these two locations for his map and drawing the right most line of retreat from Ford B.

Later when I returned to my room after this visit, I used the compass readings to determine two things: first, the heading to locate the position H of the missing twenty-eight troopers of Company E, and second, to determine the first body location on the left most line of retreat on the Maguire map.

I received permission to visit the Deep Ravine and the Keogh/Company I line of markers on Wednesday April 6 from Chief Ranger Michael Stops. On Thursday April 7, I began the most crucial day of my visit. Park Ranger Jerry Jasmer was assigned to escort me and we proceeded to the Deep Ravine. In my reading of the Reno Court of Inquiry and reviewing the Maguire map, I felt I had a good idea of where to look for the missing twenty-eight troopers.

In 1996, a team performed a ground radar search of the Deep Ravine in an attempt to locate the missing troopers. A report was prepared. The results came up empty. When I looked at the portion of the Deep Ravine they searched, I felt it did not match the area denoted on the Maguire map. Jerry Jasmer pointed out that over the years the Maguire map has been criticized as being inaccurate and not usable for analysis purposes.

I disagreed as the drawn lines were specific and changed angles at precise points. The points where the lines changed were where trooper bodies were found on June 27, 1876. When I drew my compass headings from my previous day's trek onto a copy of the Maguire map, I determined that the line drawn from where the Company C Finkle/Finley markers to H matched a 285/105 bearing. Lieutenant Maguire seemed to purposely exaggerate the Deep Ravine where it made a Y intersection. I had looked at an overhead picture of the Deep Ravine and thought I could see the Y Maguire referenced.

As Jerry Jasmer and I walked into the ravine I took a number of pictures. I took a compass reading from where we stood to where the Company C markers in the distance could be seen. The reading on my compass showed roughly 100/105 degrees or 280/285 degrees on the reverse bearing. Bingo. I had a match.

Here are some of the pictures I took while in the Deep Ravine.

The Deep Ravine before descending into the low area. Note the two mounds in the center of the picture. The Company C markers on which I took compass bearings are on the high ground to the left in this picture.

Here is one of the mounds as I walked by it. The distant trees to the left are by the visitor center.

Here is the Deep Ravine with the visitor center in the background, taken from the Greasy Grass Ridge side of the ravine. Note the mound in the center.

This is the portion of the Deep Ravine that leads to the Little Bighorn River from the Y intersection, which I explored.

After this two-hour exploration, Park Ranger Jerry Jasmer and I returned to the visitor center for a brief rest. I then prepared for the final portion of the permit exploration. The premise of my book has Lieutenant- Colonel Custer being critically wounded at Ford B during the Yates battalion attack. I needed to confirm Captain Myles Keogh's position during the battle.

Captain Keogh was the senior officer behind Custer on the northern battlefield. He would have needed to be in a position to command not only his Company I, but also provide battalion command to Company L. I wanted to see where his marker lay and judge the terrain near it to see if in fact he could act in a command fashion.

I wished to determine the battle line direction to see if the direction of Indian pressure came from Crazy Horse Ravine/ Highway 212. The markers as they lie today show a long extended line from Calhoun Hill to just short of Last Stand Hill. A few stories have the troopers rushing from the Calhoun Hill to Last Stand Hill as a last desperate retreat. To me, and to Second Lieutenant Edgerly at the Reno Court of Inquiry, the line looked like a long defensive line.

This is the line of markers for Company I and a portion of Company L. The 7th Cavalry Memorial is on the distant rise. Highway 212/Crazy Horse Ravine is to the right of this picture.

These are the markers to the extreme right of the long line of markers for Company I. Captain Myles Keogh fell here amongst a group of troopers. This area today has nineteen markers. In the immediate background is the near ridge from which Company I refused the line to the location of the markers seen in the previous picture. The command to refuse the line meant keeping Company L in position while the men of Company I bent the line rearward on the left. In this way Company I changed the direction they were facing as the new threat from Crazy Horse appeared. On the other side of the distant ridge is the Deep Coulee from which Gall and his warriors attacked.

As I walked the Captain Keogh area, I noted that markers to the right of this position were in the swale from which the Company I and Company L horses were kept. At the top of the rise were the markers of Lieutenants Calhoun and Crittenden. Captain Keogh would have been able to see them from his marker position.

Park Ranger Jasmer pointed out to me that the marker for First Sergeant Edwin Bobo from Company C was in the group about Captain Keogh. Bobo's marker placement was identified by his friend Sergeant Kanipe. Kanipe eventually married Bobo's widow. Bobo's dead horse was found on the vacant ridge beyond the Keogh marker.

Apparently, Sergeant Bobo made a dash toward the east when Company C was falling to the Indian-observed mass suicide. He chose to ride over Battle Ridge in an apparent escape attempt. Lieutenant Harrington, Sergeant Butler, and Corporal Foley made a dash to the south and southeast. Bobo's marker is shown as "Unknown" but Kanipe identified the marker to the extreme left of the nineteen markers about Captain Keogh.

This is the Sergeant Bobo marker as identified by Sergeant Kanipe and today by the park rangers.

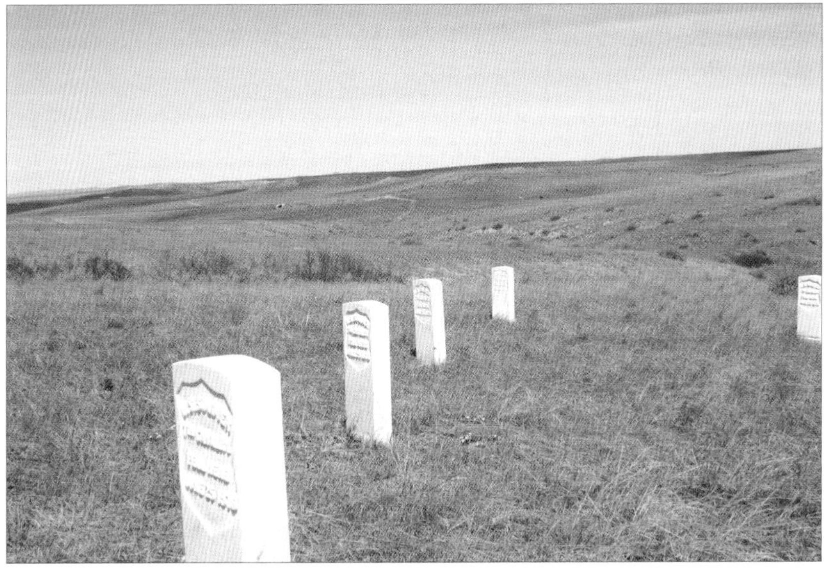

The Bobo marker is the last in this line of four markers. There were nineteen markers in this area of the Company I battlefield, near Captain Keogh. Bobo's horse was found to the right, on the next ridge.

As I returned to the park road I took time to note the Company I battle line. The markers stretched nearly to the 7th Cavalry Monument. However, I noted that there was a break in the line of markers. When I looked on the other side of the road, I found nine trooper markers. Five were near the ridge top by the road and four stretched out toward the Last Stand Hill.

My take is that with Company I falling to great Indian pressure, these nine men ran the 130 yards I measured from the battle line to the top of the ridge. This was their vain hope to escape the extreme fire of the Indians. When they topped the ridge they were confronted by the Southern Cheyenne warriors of Lame White Man. Five troopers made a stand and died. Four tried running to the group of Last Stand Hill soldiers.

In this picture, the markers of the extreme left Company I troopers can be seen. A gap existed between these markers and those of the majority of Company I to the right.

On the other side of the ridge were the nine markers that seemed to match the gap in the Company I line. Five were killed from where this picture was taken, while these four markers pointed to a rush to Last Stand Hill. Lame White Man's marker and Noisy Walking's marker were down the hill (to the left in this picture) from where the five trooper markers are found.

I made one last visit to the Ford B area to locate the point at which Maguire's map indicated a trooper died while retreating on foot. This is along the left dotted line of the Maguire map. At the Reno Court of Inquiry the first body found was located near the Ford B, over a "slight rise." It was recorded that this first trooper looked to have died while using the low rise as a defensive position. I used my compass again to explore the area. No marker headstones were in this area. But as I walked to the only slight rise as described, I found a pile of rocks. These rocks were in the position on which Lieutenant Maguire changed his dotted line toward the Company C Finley/Finkle position. I took a picture of the rocks and that position relative to the Ford B bluff.

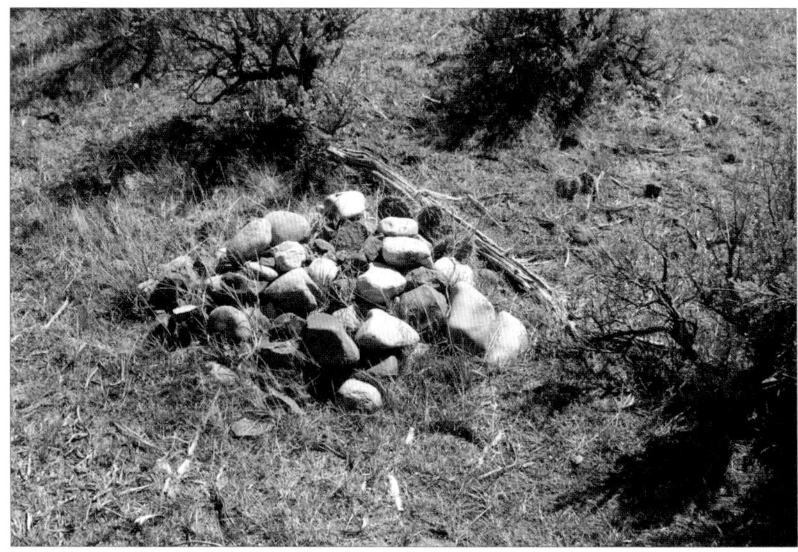

These are the rocks I found while checking this area of the Maguire map.There should have been a trooper marker near here.

The pile of rocks was located behind the small rise in front. The Ford B location, the base of the bluff on the left, and the Park Service road are seen in the background.

I finished my trip with a visit to the fenced area of Last Stand Hill. The black painted marker of General George Custer always draws the most views. For me however, the marker to the left of the dark marker, that of Captain Thomas Ward Custer, drew my attention. From the Indian memories, the last man standing was wearing a buckskin uniform with the "silver bars" of a captain. This must have been Captain Thomas Ward Custer.

Here is the marker that denotes where General George Custer's body was found.

Nearby his brother, Captain Thomas Ward Custer was found. He was the last man to fall on Last Stand Hill.

Here the men about the Custers fell. Most were from Company F, led by Captain George Yates. In the distance can be seen the Deep Ravine, in which Company E men perished.

In 1991, Congress changed the name of the battlefield to the Little Bighorn Battlefield to acknowledge the sacrifices of the American Indian participants. The Indian Memorial adjacent to the Trooper Memorial was dedicated on June 25, 2003.

This is the 7th Cavalry Memorial, under which lies the bodies of most of the fallen troopers who died during the battle. The Indian Memorial is seen in the background.

As a final tribute from me, I had with me the dirt from the barracks at Fort Lincoln. I sprinkled some at various locations where troopers had died. First was at the Custer Museum where an unknown trooper lies in front of the museum. Next, I sprinkled some at the marker designating where troopers fell at the Reno-Benteen site. I sprinkled some in the Deep Ravine for those men who still remain missing. I sprinkled some on the Keogh battle line. Lastly, I sprinkled some at the 7th Cavalry Memorial.

These troopers were all from some family, somewhere. They died as Unknowns, away from home, family, and friends. To symbolically help their spirits rest easier, I brought some of their last home, Fort Lincoln, to them.

I took soil from the Keogh battle line. On my way back to Minnesota, I once again stopped at Fort Lincoln. I walked back to the same barracks and sprinkled the soil from the Little Bighorn. The once blood-stained soil, the soil on which these troopers died and breathed their last, was returned to their home. My mission was complete.

And with that final act, I returned to my home, to my family. My tale, and the story of the Little Bighorn I believe to be true, will always be uncertain. As Park Ranger Jerry Jasmer and I wrapped up my visit in his office, he still believed that George Armstrong Custer was in charge to the end. I had walked the ground with him, and I said I still believed my story to be accurate.

More than 5000 stories and books have been written on the subject. To this day no one story seems to dominate. Either Custer was one of the last to die, or *Custer Went First*. I offered to Jerry a polite resolution to this dilemma. I would flip a coin and either two out of three, or four out of seven times to determine Custer's fate. Another staff member heard the comment and laughed. Jerry and I laughed. We shook hands and I thanked Jerry and the staff for the wonderful week I shared while in their presence.

Park Ranger Jerry Jasmer and me as we finished my week at the Little Bighorn National Battlefield. I owe much thanks and gratitude to this fine public servant, historian of the battle, and one of the nicest people one will ever meet anywhere.

Appendix A

Army Casualties Killed or missing at the Battles of the Little Bighorn, June 25 - 26, 1876.

Per Exhibit No. 6 of the Reno Court Of Inquiry

Company	Name	Rank
Field/Staff	George A. Custer	Lt. Col./ Bvt. Maj. Gen.
	W. W. Cooke	Lt./ Bvt. Lt. Col.
	Lord	Asst. Surg.
	J. M. DeWolf	Act'g Asst. Surg.
N. C. Staff	W. W. Sharrow	Sergt. Maj.
	Henry Voss	Chief Trptr.
A Co.	Henry Dalious	Corpl.
	George H. King	Corpl.
	John E. Armstrong	Pvt.
	James Drinan	Pvt.
	William Moody	Pvt.
	James McDonald	Pvt.
	Richard Rawlins	Pvt.
	John Sullivan	Pvt.
	Thomas P. Switzer	Pvt.
B Co.	Benj. Hodgson	2nd Lt.
	Richard Doran	Pvt.
	George Mack	Pvt.

C Co.	Thomas Ward Custer	Capt./ Bvt. Lt. Col.
	H. M. Harrington	2nd Lt.
	Edwin Bobo	1st Sergt.
	Finley	Sergt.
	Finkle	Sergt.
	French	Corpl.
	Foley	Corpl.
	Ryan	Corpl.
	Allen	Pvt.
	Criddle	Pvt.
	King	Pvt.
	Bucknell	Pvt.
	Eisman	Pvt.
	Engle	Pvt.
	Brightfield	Pvt.
	Farrand	Pvt.
	Griffin	Pvt.
	Hawel	Pvt.
	Hattisoll	Pvt.
	Kingsoutz	Pvt.
	Lewis	Pvt.
	Mayer	Pvt.
	Mayer	Pvt.
	Phillips	Pvt.
	Russell	Pvt.
	Rix	Pvt.
C	Rauter	Pvt.
	Short	Pvt.
	Shea	Pvt.
	Shade	Pvt.
	Stuart	Pvt.
	St. John	Pvt.
	Thadius	Pvt.
	Van Allen	Pvt.
	Warren	Pvt.
	Wyndham	Pvt.
	Wright	Pvt.

D Co.	Vincent Charlie	Farrier
	Patrick Golden	Pvt.
	Edward Hansen	Pvt.
E Co.	A. E. Smith	1st Lt./ Bvt. Capt.
	J. Sturgis	2nd Lt.
	Fred Hohmeyer	1st Sergt.
	Ogden	Sergt.
	James	Sergt.
	Hagan	Corpl.
	Mason	Corpl.
	Blorn (Brown?)	Corpl.
	Meyer	Corpl.
	McElroy	Trpt.
	Mooney	Trptr.
E	Baker	Pvt.
	Boyle	Pvt.
	Bauth	Pvt.
	Connor	Pvt.
	Darring	Pvt.
	Davis	Pvt.
	Farrell	Pvt.
	Hiley	Pvt.
	Huber	Pvt.
	Hime	Pvt.
	Henderson	Pvt.
	Henderson	Pvt.
	Leddison	Pvt.
	O'Connor	Pvt.
	Rood	Pvt.
	Reese	Pvt.
	Smith 1st	Pvt.
	Smith 2nd	Pvt.
	Smith 3rd	Pvt.
	Stella	Pvt.
	Smallwood	Pvt.
	Tarr	Pvt.

	VanSant	Pvt.
	Walker	Pvt.
	Brogen	Pvt.
	Knicht	Pvt.

F Co.	G. W. Yates	Capt.
	W. Van Reilly	2nd Lt.
	Kenney	1st Sergt.
	Nursey	Sergt.
	Vickory	Sergt.
	Wilkinson	Sergt.
	Colman	Corpl.
	Teeman	Corpl.
	Briody	Corpl.
	Brandon	Farrier
	Manning	Blacksmith
	Atchison	Pvt.
	Brown 1st	Pvt.
	Brown 2nd	Pvt.
	Bruce	Pvt.
	Brady	Pvt.
	Burnham	Pvt.
	Cather	Pvt.
	Carney	Pvt.
	Dohman	Pvt.
	Donnelly	Pvt.
	Gardiner	Pvt.
	Hammon	Pvt.
	Kline	Pvt.
	Knauth	Pvt.
	Luman	Pvt.
	Losse	Pvt.
	Milton Jos	Pvt.
	Madson	Pvt.
	Monroe	Pvt.

F	Audden	Pvt.
	Omeling	Pvt.
	Sicfus	Pvt.

	Warren	Pvt.
	Way	Pvt.
	Lerock	Pvt.
	Kelley	Pvt.
G Co.	Donald McIntosh	1st Lt.
	Edward Botzer	Sergt.
	M. Considine	Sergt.
	Jas. Martin	Corpl.
	Otto Hageman	Corpl.
	Benj. Wells	Farrier
	Henry Dose	Trptr.
	Crawford Selby	Saddler
	Benj. F. Magers	Pvt.
	Andrew J. Moore	Pvt.
	John J. McGinniss	Pvt.
	Edward Stanley	Pvt.
	Henry Seafferman	Pvt.
	John Rapp	Pvt.
H Co.	Geo. Lell	Corpl.
	Julian D. Jones	Corpl.
	Thos. E. Meador	Corpl.
I Co.	M. W. Keogh	Capt./ Bvt. Lt. Col.
	J. E. Porter	1st Lt.t
	F. E. Varden	1st Sergt.
	J. Bustard	Sergt.
	John Wild	Corpl.
	G. C. Morris	Corpl.
	S. F. Staples	Corpl.
	J. McGucker	Trptr.
	J. Patton	Trptr.
	H. A. Bailey	Blacksmith
	J. F. Broadhurst	Pvt.
	J. Barry	Pvt.
	J. Connors	Pvt.
	T. P. Downing	Pvt.

	E. C. Driscoll	Pvt.
	D. C. Gillette	Pvt.
	G. H. Cross	Pvt.
	E. P. Holcomb	Pvt.
	M. E. Horn	Pvt.
	Adam Hetismer	Pvt.
	P. Kelley	Pvt.
	Fred Lehman	Pvt.
	Henry Lehman	Pvt.
	E. P. Lloyd	Pvt.
	A. McIlhargey	Pvt.
	J. Mitchell	Pvt.
	J. Noshang	Pvt.
	J. O'Bryan	Pvt.
	J. Parker	Pvt.
	F. J. Pitter	Pvt.
I	Geo. Post	Pvt.
	Jas. Quinn	Pvt.
	William Reed	Pvt.
	J. W. Rossbury	Pvt.
	S. L. Symms	Pvt.
	J. E. Troy	Pvt.
	Chas. VonBramer	Pvt.
	W. B. Whaley	Pvt.
K Co.	D. Winney	1st Sergt.
	R. Hughes	Sergt.
	J. J. Callahan	Corpl.
	Julius Helmer	Trptr.
	Eli U. T. Clair	Pvt.
L Co.	James Calhoun	1st Lt.
	J. J. Crittenden	Lt. 20th Inf.
	Butler	1st Sergt.
	Warren	Sergt.
	Harrison	Corpl.
	Gilbert	Corpl.

	Seiller	Corpl.
	Walsh	Corpl.
	Adams	Trumpeter
	Adams	Pvt.
	Assdely	Pvt.
	Burke	Pvt.
	Cheever	Pvt.
	McGill	Pvt.
	McCarthy	Pvt.
L	Dugan	Pvt.
	Maxwell	Pvt.
	Scott	Pvt.
	Babcock	Pvt.
	Perkins	Pvt.
	Tarbox	Pvt.
	Dye	Pvt.
	Tessier	Pvt.
	Galvin	Pvt.
	Graham	Pvt.
	Hamilton	Pvt.
	Rodgers	Pvt.
	Snow	Pvt.
	Hughes	Pvt.
	Miller	Pvt.
	Tweed	Pvt.
	Vetter	Pvt.
	Cashan	Pvt.
	Keefe	Pvt.
	Andrews	Pvt.
	Crisfield	Pvt.
	Harrington	Pvt.
	Haugge	Pvt.
	Kavanaugh	Pvt.
	Lobering	Pvt.
	Mahoney	Pvt.
	Schmidt	Pvt.
	Simon	Pvt.
	Semenson	Pvt.
	Riebold	Pvt.

L	O'Connell	Pvt.
M Co.	Miles F. O'Hara	Sergt.
	Henry M. Scollin	Corpl.
	Fred Stringer	Corpl. "
	Henry Gordon	Pvt.
	H. Klotzbrusher	Pvt.
	G. Lawrence	Pvt.
	W. D. Meyer	Pvt.
	G. E. Smith	Pvt.
	D. Somers	Pvt.
	J. Tanner	Pvt.
	H. Turley	Pvt.
	H. C. Vogt	Pvt.
Civilians	Boston Custer	
	Arthur Reed	
	Mark Kellogg	
	Chas. Reynolds.	
	Frank C. Mann	
Indian Scouts	Bloody Knife	
	Bobtailed Bull	
	Stab	

Appendix B

Indian Casualties

Indian Warriors Killed at the Battles of the Little Bighorn, June 25-26 Per Interviews with Survivors As Told To David Humphreys Miller

Tribe	Name
Hunkpapa	Swift Bear
	White Buffalo
	Long Road
	Hawk Man
	Rectum (Guts)
	Red Face
Sans Arcs	Two Bears
	Standing Elk
	Long Robe
	Long Dog
	Elk Bear
	Cloud Man
	Kills-Him

Two Kettle	Chased-By-Owls
Oglala	White Eagle Many Lice Bad-Light-Hair Young Skunk Black White Man
Cheyenne	Whirlwind Left Hand Owns-Red-Horse Black Cloud, Flying By Bearded Man (Mustache) Swift Cloud Noisy Walking Limber Bones Hump Nose Black Bear Lame White Man
Minneconjou	High Horse Long Elk

Bibliography

Ambrose, Stephen E. *Crazy Horse and Custer, The Parallel Lives of Two American Warriors*. New York: Meridian, the Penguin Group, Penguin Books, Inc., 1975.

Brown, Dee. *Bury My Heart At Wounded Knee*. New York: Henry Holt and Company, 1970.

Brown, Jesse, and A. M. Willard. *The Black Hills Trails -Peter Thompson's Story of the Battle of the Little Bighorn*. Rapid City, SD: Rapid City Journal Co., 1924. www.astonisher.com, 2009.

Camp, Walter Mason. *Custer in '76: Walter Camp's Notes on the Custer Fight*, 1908. Edited by Kenneth Hammer. Brigham Young University Press. 1976. www.astonisher.com, 2009.

Camp, Walter Mason. *John Martin's Story of the Battle, A 7th Cavalry Survivor's Account of the Battle of the Little Bighorn*, 1908. Edited by Kenneth Hammer. Brigham Young University Press. 1976. www.astonisher.com, 2009.

Carley, Kenneth. *The Dakota War of 1862, Minnesota's Other Civil War*. St. Paul, MN: Minnesota Historical Society Press, 1961, 1976.

Coffeen, Herbert. *The Custer Battle Book - Hairy Moccasin's Story of the Battle*. New York: Carlton Press, Inc., 1964. www.astonisher.com, 2009.

Connell, Evan S. *Son Of The Morning Star, Custer and the Little Bighorn*. New York: HarperCollins Publishers, 1984.

Cooke, Philip St. George. *The 1862 U.S. Cavalry Tactics.* originally published U.S. Government Printing Office, Washington, D.C., 1862. Republished Mechanicsburg, PA: Stackpole Books, 2004.

Custer, George A. *My Life On The Plains.* New York: Sheldon and Co., 1874.

Donovan, James. *A Terrible Glory, Custer and the Little Bighorn, The Last Great Battle of the American West.* New York: Bay Back Books, Little, Brown and Company, 2008.

Gwynne, S. C.*Empire of the Summer Moon.* New York: Scribner, a Division of Simon and Schuster, Inc., 2010.

Graham, Col. W. A. *The Custer Myth: A Source Book of Custerania - Daniel Kanipe's Story of the Battle of the Little Bighorn.* Harrisburg, PA: The Stackpole Co., 1953. www.astonisher.com, 2009.

Graham, Col. W. A. *The Custer Myth: A Source Book of Custerania -White Man Runs Him"s Story of the Battle of the Little Bighorn..* Harrisburg, PA: The Stackpole Co., 1953. www.astonisher.com, 2009.

Graham, Col. W. A., "The Official Record of a Court Of Inquiry convened at Chicago, Illinois, January 13, 1879, by The President of the United States upon the request of Major Marcus A. Reno, 7th U. S. Cavalry to investigate his conduct at the battle of the Little Big Horn, June 25-26, 1876," *The 1879 Reno Court Of Inquiry*. Pacific Palisades, CA. 1951.

Grant, Ulysses, S. *The Personal Memoirs of U. S. Grant.* Acheron Press, 1885.

Hedren, Paul L.*The Great Sioux War 1876-77 -The Best From Montana:The Magazine of Western History.* Helena: Montana Historical Society Press, 1991.

Johnston, Terry C. *A Cold Day In Hell- The Dull Knife Battle, 1876.* New York: Bantam Books, 1996.

Johnston, Terry C. *Long Winter Gone.*, New York: Bantam Books, 1990.

Johnston, Terry C. *Reap The Whirlwind.*, New York: Bantam Books, 1994.

Johnston, Terry C. *Seize The Sky*. New York: Bantam Books, 1991.

Johnston, Terry C. *Sioux Dawn.* , New York: St. Martin's Press, 1990.

Johnston, Terry C. *Trumpet On The Land*. New York: Bantam Books, 1995.

Johnston, Terry C. *Turn The Stars Upside Down*. New York: St. Martin's Press, 2001.

Johnston, Terry C. *Wolf Mountain Moon*. New York: Bantam Books, 1997.

Lamar, Howard R. *The New Encyclodedia of the American West*. Yale University Press, HarpersCollins Publishers, Inc., 1977.

Miller, David Humphreys. *Custer's Fall - The Native American Side of the Story.* New York: Meridan - Penguin Putnam, Inc., 1957, 1992.

Miller, David Humphreys, "*Echoes of the Little Bighorn - White Cow Bull's Story of the Battle*. American Heritage, 1971. www.astonisher.com, 2009.

Philbrick, Nathaniel. *The Last Stand -Custer, Sitting Bull, and the Battle of the Little Bighorn.*, New York: Viking, Penguin Group, 2010.

Rickey, Don and McChristian, Douglas C. *Reno-Benteen Entrenchment Trail*. Custer Battlefield Historical and Museum Association, 1992.

Terry, Alfred H. *The Field Diary of General Alfred H. Terry, The Yellowstone Expedition – 1876*. Big Byte Books, 2004.

Utley, Robert M. *Little Bighorn Battlefield* . Washington, D.C.: National Park Service, National Handbook Series no. 1, 1969.

Utley, Robert M. *Custer Battlefield – Official National Park Handbook*. Washington, D.C.: Division of Publications, National Park Service, U.S. Dept. of the Interior, 1988.

Picture Sources:

All picture illustrations in this book are from the collection of the author, Kerry G. Lundmark, except the following:

- Cover image of Captain Yates: Courtesy of the National Park Service, Little Bighorn Battlefield National Monument, LIBI_00015_00605, Photographed by J. N. Choate, "Drawing of Captain George Yates in Dress Uniform," circa, 1868.
- Cover image of Captain Myles Keogh: Courtesy of the National Park Service, Little Bighorn Battlefield National Monument, LIBI_00015_00592, Photographed by E. Klauber, "Myles W. Keogh in Bust View," date unknown.
- P. 209 – 210, Aerial photos: Courtesy of the USGS.
- Map images of Maguire Map: Courtesy of the U. S. Army Corps of Engineers. (public domain).
- Map images from the Reno Court of Inquiry: Courtesy of the University of Wisconsin. (public domain).